"In a conversational style, Heather Vargas has written a tender, honest, vulnerable account of how she found a way to live life with purpose after the devastating loss of her two-year-old daughter, Emma. Heather does not provide a magic fix, nor does she promise a quick solution. Instead, she walks you through her struggles to find peace after an unimaginable tragedy. Let your tears fall freely as you find healing and restoration through the words of a grieving mother who has written what many of us who have experienced enormous loss have felt deep inside, and may you know that there is life and hope after death and despair."

Keith Hood, Senior Pastor
Harvest Community Church

"Heather Vargas takes us beyond the norm of a clinical review of the important and relevant topic of grief. She speaks directly from her own heart, to the heart of the person struggling from the loss of a loved one. Her words provide tremendous perspective to those of us who seek to have a healing influence on those struggling in this way."

Paul Weissenborn, Lead Pastor
River Oak Grace Community Church

BLM

A journey through life, loss, and hope

Heather Vargas

A journey through life, loss, and hope
Heather Vargas

BLOOM

For information contact: Shalako Press
P.O. Box 371, Oakdale, CA 95361-0371
http://www.shalakopress.com

ISBN: 978-0-9846811-2-9

Cover design: Heather Vargas
Cover photographs: Anna Mayer
Cover format: Karen Borrelli
Editor: Daphne Eck - daphnedel.com

PRINTED IN THE UNITED STATES OF AMERICA

BLⓄⓄM

Table of Contents

Introduction
- The events that have led to the place I have found myself in
- A legacy passed down
- Our little "Amazing Grace"
- The Strength of a man- Some words from Emma's dad

Part 1- Suffering

- Saying good-bye
- The community embraces us
- The First Year
- Grieving and raising kids
- Distraction lightens the load
- Irrational thoughts; Irrational moments
- Life's not Fair…Loss comes in many forms

Part 2- Faith

- God prepares us- His undeniable presence
- Why do bad things happen to good people?
- Why would God allow this if He loves you?
- Do you just have "blind faith" no matter what?
- God hurt my feelings!
- What staying mad at God really means
- Do you believe good will ultimately come out of this tragedy?
- Not my will, but Thine
- Initial Prayers and Journal Entries

Part 3- Choices

- Quite simply, will you choose despair or will you choose peace?
- How do you go to work and carry on?
- Where does your strength come from?
- Choices today will affect our tomorrows
- Making choices based on mind instead of emotions
- A grieving wife
- Be realistic about what you are grieving for
- Happiness is a choice
- Corporate grief, anti-depressants, and going crazy

Part 4- Healing

- New buds emerge
- Comforts and difficulties
- What does a grieving person look like?
- The meaning of Christmas revealed
- Giving to others
- Do you relive that night daily? Do you have regret, guilt or blame?
- Gluttony, Rebellion, and feeling sorry for myself
- I have healed, but it is not over

Part 5- Restoration and Hope

- I do not have to be defined by my pain
- Finding my place
- Special days and keeping their memory alive
- Facing the future
- Acceptance and Hope- Your loved one's legacy
- Living Large
- Because He Lives
- In Full Bloom

Closing and Reflection

Matt,
Although we did not sign up for this journey, I feel blessed
to be on it with you. Your steadfast faith and trust in God has
helped to sustain me. Your belief that this would be made
right reminds me that it is not about me. Thank you for
trusting God and for leading our family.

Tyler and Jayden,
You are the most incredible boys in the world! Emma could
have never been given two greater brothers! I'm sorry that
you have been entrusted with this incredible burden of grief
at such young ages. I'm sure that God is equipping you both
for something great one day through this. You have given me
a deeper calling to live and to be joyful once again. Thank
you for being awesome and for always making me proud!

Emma,
You brought this world more sunshine in your two short
years than many who live long lives. You have fulfilled your
purpose here on earth and your legacy will continue to
inspire others to shine their lights! I am proud to call you my
daughter and there is only one you, beautiful you. I miss you
and my hearts tugs for you. Thank you for inspiring me to
write this book in your memory. Mommy loves you!

Prelude

This book has become a collection of thoughts, journal entries, and prayers during my grieving process. Although at first I felt exposed to share such intimate moments, I ultimately recognized it as the thing God calls us to do.

"Rejoice with them that rejoice, and weep with them that weep" Romans 12:15

I began sensing a need for this book as I continued to encounter the same questions regarding my grief… How do you do it? Where does your strength come from? How come you're not mad at God? Why do bad things happen? The question/answer format of this book was developed by questions that people would ask me. Although I do not feel like I have all of the answers to some of these very complex questions, I do have thoughts that have taken me from a place of desperation to a place of peace. You will also find that the format of this book is topical rather than chronological with the exception of the introduction.

I hope that you find a balance in this book of both faith and psychology. I believe that there is enough room for faith and trust to exist side by side with disappointment, anger and sadness. My experience in reading books on grief is that the messages would fall on either side of faith or psychology. Our mind is powerful and we make choices every day. We also have a powerful God who gives us strength if we trust Him. My hope is that all who read this will be inspired to discover how they can live rich lives despite life's circumstances. Life is hard sometimes. In our hard moments, we have the ability to shine more than ever if we choose to.

Introduction

"Home is where your story begins"

A life in bloom had found me. I had it all. I was raised by two wonderful parents, Danny and Terry Holcomb. I had a husband who adored me and three beautiful kids. I started teaching when I was just 21 years old. I had great friends and I built my life in a small town. We lived in a cozy house and we designed a pool for our backyard. I had the *good life*…until July 6, 2010.

Matt and I were young when we met. I was 17 and he was 20. We met on a blind date of sorts. We dated for five years and were married in 1996. Being the planners that we are, we decided to wait five years to begin a family. We did just that. While visiting my parents in Texas for Christmas, I began to feel sick. When we got back to California, we found out that I was expecting a baby. About 8 weeks into my pregnancy, I went for a routine ultrasound, but the baby didn't look good. I had a miscarriage. I had a D and C weeks later. I thought this would be my "test" in life and I was determined to posture myself correctly. "This baby was not meant to be…and on and on." "I would praise God in this storm"…I had no idea of the storms that were to come.

In August of the following year, I was pregnant again. We were overjoyed. As fate would have it, I contracted Fifth disease which only poses a threat if you're pregnant. I was sent to see a genetic specialist every three weeks. I had to get counseling to prepare myself in case something went wrong with the baby. Fortunately, everything went fine and our first son Tyler Mathew was born on May 9, 2001. He was such a blessing to us! Tyler was an easy baby and he just loved everything. (He is still like that!) Tyler was and is a typical first born. He exceeded all of his developmental stages and of course we thought he was the cutest and smartest baby we had ever seen. He has continued to thrive and he is a smart, funny character who loves sports, music and books. We are very blessed to call him our son.

Matt and I decided to wait three years before our next baby. We did. I had experienced morning sickness with Tyler, so I thought I'd plan my first trimester during the summer so I wouldn't have to work during that time. I did. I was sick during the summer of 2003, and Jayden Michael was born on February 10, 2004. I went to the hospital to be induced with Jayden on February 9th, but Jayden then and now has always done things in his own time. He was born early the next morning. He was a peanut. Jayden was the perfect addition to our family. Tyler embraced the role of "big brother" naturally and life was good. Jayden was a quieter, more cautious baby and he still is. He is very smart, but understated. He loves art, excels in sports and enjoys spending time with his friends. Again, we feel blessed to call him our son.

I was happy to be the mother of boys, but I always thought I'd have girls. I had begun to embrace the idea of boys and all that they bring. I remember a card that my dad gave me that said, "Heather, God knows what you need, and He knows what it is best." It gave me the assurance that God has called me to be the mother of sons, and I still remember that advice when my spirit is not settled.

My first real heartbreak came in 2004 when my dad was diagnosed with cancer. Our family knew that God would provide a miracle and heal my dad. He did not. When my dad had received the news that he had months to live in May of 2005, I asked him if he was scared. He said, "No. If God is calling me home, God is calling me home. I would've liked to live at least to 60; Just promise me that you'll take care of your mom…She is a saint." Even when he was dying, he was thinking of someone else. What a life lesson. My dad went to be with Jesus on May 22, 2005; six days (not months) after his terminal diagnosis. My mom was 50 without her husband; my sisters and I were 30, 27, and 16 without our dad, and my sons and nieces and nephew without their "papa". Life didn't seem fair.

I struggled with this loss for at least 2 years. I questioned God. I fought God. I tried to find contradictions in the bible. During my rant, I was humbled. I learned that it is not about me (The title of Max Lucado's book that my dad was reading on his deathbed). Pastor Rick Murray, our small group leader at the time, taught me, reminded me, and was patient with me. In the end I learned that God is God and I am not. With a renewed passion to serve, to bless and be blessed, life had resumed. My sons Tyler and Jayden were tots on the move. Two years had passed and Matt and I were contemplating another baby. A couple of weeks into

September, I started to experience some of those all too familiar symptoms. We were elated! I wrapped my head around our new bundle of joy immediately. The boys were excited and cautious of our new addition. Needless to say, Matt was through the moon! The practical side in me knew that another boy would be easy, but that a little girl would be such a treat!

A wee bit of heaven drifted down from Above.

We went to "Womb with a View" on Matt's birthday, a crisp December day. As the woman who was helping us was administering the sonogram, she said, "Yep, I'm 100% sure." All I could see were these two circles that I thought were "boy goods". I started sweating! Matt was sweating. The boys were nervous. She said, "It's a girl!" and the boys both burst into tears! Matt and I were so happy, but we were trying to console the boys!

I couldn't believe my ears! A little girl in our home! How foreign! How exciting! Because it was the holiday season, we decided to stop off at the mall. My first instinct was to run in and buy something PINK of course, but the boys, especially Tyler, had somber faces. I decided not to act too excited or squeal when I saw pink. After all, I said time and time again, that this was a baby coming into our home, not a princess. A baby is a baby is a baby. I later realized what that was all about. I think the boys were unsure of what a girl would do to the rankings in our house. They knew how we treated boys, they knew there was enough love, but this idea of a girl threatened their security. These feelings didn't last long, though.

Just as my pregnancy with Emma was easy and uneventful, her birth was the same- The easiest of all of my children. From the moment they handed her to me, life was just easy and good. She was barely 6 pounds, a little petite thing. She was born and blessed with an easy-going personality. So just like that, everything was new, different and better than we imagined. Emma Grace Vargas was born on May 15, 2008. We left the hospital with her on my birthday, May 17th and we all felt so good we went out for Mexican food! We also ran into Mervyn's so I could buy a "tummy tucker" because I was to be in Matt's sister Dianne's wedding in a few weeks…and a girl's gotta do what a girl's gotta do! The clerk asked, "How old is your baby?" We all just looked at each other and laughed…uh 48 hours!? We all felt great! I felt like God had blessed our family. There was a renewed spirit in our whole family and we were all smiling once again. Emma was extraordinary in that she was so easy, a doll, and very smart. We knew her potential was endless and we all just marveled in watching to see who she would become. I was introduced to a "pink" load of laundry, dolls, hair bows, and a mini-me. Indeed we had it all…until that night.

That Night

On July 6th 2010, we all had attended Tyler's first all-star baseball game. We were all dressed in purple to support his team. Emma was wearing purple capris, a striped purple shirt, and a purple bow. She even had a purple sippy cup! (We were sometimes a bit overboard) An afternoon just like so many others.

Tyler lost the game and he was devastated. Matt, Jayden and Emma ran the bases around the field after the game, and I snapped some pictures.

When we got home, Tyler went to his room, sad. Jayden asked Matt if he would help him type a letter to Tyler letting him know that he is an all-star anyhow. I was going to be cooking dinner and Matt was going to watch the kids. The kitchen was silent, unusually silent, and with all that is within me, I believed that Emma was in our room with Matt and Jayden because the door was closed and she wasn't with me.

While I was making tacos, our dog scratched on the backdoor to get out. I cracked the door open because I thought Emma was with Matt. Even once the dog returned, I had a heightened sense of awareness and I scanned the backyard. I looked in Emma's playhouse; I looked where the dog went to the bathroom. I wasn't looking for Emma per se, but I was eminently aware of my surroundings. I let the dog in and shut the backdoor. Then Matt and Jayden opened the bedroom door and came into the kitchen. I immediately said, "Where is Emma?" He said, "I thought she was with you!" We both panicked and ran to the backdoor, and there she was face down in the water near the steps. How could this be possible? Less than five minutes prior I looked in the pool and scanned the whole backyard. Matt pulled her out and I being a lifeguard began CPR on my baby. Matt called 911. It was surreal. This couldn't really be happening. But it was.

We remained surprisingly calm because we did not want to further frighten the boys. A neighbor came over and took the boys and a paramedic that was visiting across the street took over for me.

Matt made phone calls to family and I just paced around my daughter. I cried, "C'mon baby, you can do it". But she was already gone. We both knew it, but we were going to hold on to any shred of hope we could. Paramedics came. Police questioned us. A medi-flight landed by our house.

Damn-it! How could this be happening? So, off we head to the hospital. We weren't allowed to ride in the ambulance. I was sick the entire drive; I desperately wanted to be with her. We arrived to the ER with doctors and nurses surrounding our baby. I was determined to stay calm so I could stay with her, and also to not add more stress for the boys. The doctors worked on her for a couple of hours. Matt and I cried and prayed. At one time there was a faint heartbeat; a bit of hope. Finally the head doctor said, "It is finished." They took all of the cords off of her and gave her to me.

In the most horrific moment of our lives, Matt and I were both clothed in peace. I was given the wisdom to be able to hold her and look past her, and look to my boys and reassure them that our family would be ok. Matt led our family recognizing it as a test of faith and that God would give us strength. There was no screaming or thrashing, like one might imagine. I remember someone from the hospital staff telling me to let them know when I was ready. I said, "Ready for what? To leave my daughter here and go home? I'll never be ready!" But still I was calm. I held her. I stroked her hair and kissed her face. I felt like I was doing it but not really living it. The time did come where one more stroke of the hair was no different than the one before. It was time to leave. Tyler wanted to hold his sister and say good-bye. (Yikes! I was introduced to grieving and raising kids 101 in an instant!) With the last hugs and kisses on this side of eternity, we said good-bye. We were leaving the hospital in transparent bodies. It's as if we drifted to the parking lot. I noticed people looking at us, but it was as if they were not really there. I certainly did not feel like I was there. We walked to my car and I immediately noticed her car seat in the back seat. I broke. My brother-in-law Randy took the car seat out and put it in the trunk. I have a small car, but that night the back seat seemed as big as a bus with the void of Emma. We followed my mom and family to stay in Hilmar that night; we weren't prepared to go home.

Planning a funeral

Trying to sleep that first night at my mom's was hard. Physically my body was twisted and unsettled. I'm pretty sure that my heart was trying to come out of my chest. I couldn't eat anything. I didn't care about food or anything for that matter. Somehow I was able to shower and prepare to go to town to begin to make funeral arrangements. Matt and I, my mom and our friend Sandi went to Turlock Funeral Home. I kept thinking, "Am I really doing this?" "I don't want to plan a funeral for my daughter!" I knew that even with those decisions, I could be an active role in the decisions surrounding my daughter. We were greeted by a man named Ben, who offered his condolences and his services. Their business was more than generous with us and we feel forever grateful to them. Although he made our experience as good as it could be, the truth is that I was still looking to choose a "baby casket", something no one should ever have to do. We did choose one, and it was just the beginning of decisions that had to be made.

From decisions on music, to speakers, to pictures and a slideshow, I had my work cut out for me. I felt like this was the last thing, the last "party" I could throw for Emma and I wanted it perfect. I wanted everyone who attended her funeral to feel a sense of inspiration by her two short years.

Just as I thought I had finished all of the preparations, I was tucking the boys into bed, and Tyler tells me he wants to sing at her funeral! "What!" I exclaimed. "It's 9:30 at night and the music has already been worked out!" Then he became sad and I knew that the decision that would be made would stay with him forever (Raising kids and Grief 102). So I spent about two hours with him on his bed trying to figure something out. I asked him if he would like to sing with Whitney, a friend and one of the singers at the service, but he said no. He wanted to do something on his own. Then it came to me. I asked him if he would like to recite the lyrics to one of his favorite songs. Just months before, Tyler and I had attended a Sidewalk Prophets concert. The song, "The words I would say" is a song that I have dedicated to him. He agreed. So with tired eyes and broken hearts, the decision was made. His body relaxed as he needed to be able to do something for his sister. Off to bed for one of the longest days in our lives is ahead.

The Funeral

My friend Anna had some beautiful programs made with the photos she had taken of Emma. Countless others contributed to the day with photos, picture boards, pink ribbons for everyone to wear, and so much more.

As I entered the funeral home I could hardly breathe. I had prayed that seeing Emma would not leave a bad or scary impression on me or the boys. She looked just like her little self, with her pink princess nightgown on, and her favorite blanket and BB. I had intentions to keep the blanket with me after the service, but she was "tucked in" perfectly so I couldn't do it.

The walk to see Emma was met with so many flowers and plant arrangements. One in particular, a giant floral ladybug caught my eye. I rushed over to it and it took my breath away. I began to cry. It was from her preschool friends Colie, Caleb, and Bella three special children who shared their daily lives with Emma. She loved them so much and they loved her.

It was time for people to start filing in. I had asked the funeral director to keep everyone outside so I could have a few minutes alone. But soon, it was time to begin. The service flowed like a dance, a dance that had consumed me the days before. There were more than 400 people; there was standing room only. Several people only heard the service from an adjoining room due to the crowds.

In that moment, Matt and I felt so honored to be Emma's parents. We were thankful for our daughter and for all of the people who came to say good-bye to her and to support our family. We also realized that moment as a platform to begin Emma's legacy. With no pressure from us, Tyler approached the podium and had recited the lyrics to our song from memory. "Be strong in the Lord, never give up hope. You're going to do great things. I already know.

15

God's got his hands on you so don't live life in fear. Forgive and forget, but don't forget why you're here. Take your time and pray, these are the words I would say." We were proud that our son had the strength and the love to give in that moment. The community was watching. This was the first moment to shine in darkness...to portray the light that Emma was in our lives.

Although we were obviously devastated and in shock, God carried each member of our family that day and in the days to come. But I have missed Emma every day, every minute since that moment. My heart aches for her and probably always will. Tyler and Jayden miss her and speak of her often. Matt longs for his little girl. This book has been born out of all of our grief.

Grief is a unique journey. No two situations are the same; therefore no two people have the same response. The only thing I'd like to offer is a soft place to fall, peace within your spirit, and the choice to live your life in a profound way.

A Legacy Passed Down

When I think about the person that I have become, I think about the threads of my mom and dad that have been woven into my being. I (and you) are unique people aside from our parents, but the influence from them is an undeniable force that often sets our course.

Without ever really being conscious of it, I think that much of who I have become has been in an effort to respect and carry on some of my dad's amazing traits that were just part of who he was. In addition, my mom's influence is ever-present in my life and continues to inspire me.

Much of my childhood was spent living in Panama. My family moved there when I was just two years old, and stayed there until I was ten. My dad worked on the Panama Canal. Modeled there for me was the blending of cultures and respect for others. Part of the legacy passed down from both of my parents is treating all people with dignity. Panama is a very poor country, and smiles and kindness offered to others always seemed to make an impression. Service and the giving of time and money on behalf of others were never done in an effort of duty, but rather it was just in the joy of doing it. My dad learned Spanish and he never thought he was better than anyone else (although I do recall him having a velour robe that read, "Mr. Wonderful", but I digress). He made people happy when they were around him. He was a fun guy. He was easy-going and dependable. So we have this fun, happy guy on the one side, and those traits were married with faith, belief, and conviction on the other. He would often say, "You are either for God or you are against Him; there is no gray area." He was a black and white thinker when it came to faith. He taught us about the importance of God and faith. He didn't just tell us it was important, the actions in his life demonstrated it. For example, after a long commute from the bay area, he would come home and read his bible for hours. On the weekends he would go to the bible bookstore to sing and buy music. He was an ordained music minister and he spent hours singing praises. I can still hear him singing "People Need the Lord" and "I Sing Because". He was not a perfect man, but his pursuit to be who God wanted him to be was his quest. My dad loved sports, especially baseball. While living in Panama, he started a co-ed softball league and there is a field named after him, "Holcomb Field". I remember him getting the military (which he was not a part of) to help him transport barracks to use for the dugouts. He was a uniter. He brought people together.

The other influence obviously, is my mom. She was the quieter one of the two. She followed my dad as he moved (not just to cities and states, but to another country) She yielded to him as she knew that he was yielding to God. My mom was the mom that everyone wanted. My mom was the nice mom; the loving mom. I always felt safe with her. We had rules, but we just never got into much trouble and life always seemed pretty easy. She too, had a lot of friends and social outlets. Her and my dad would go on a date every week and we would have a babysitter. They always said that the best thing you can do for your children is love each other. My mom is a mercy shower, so her heart breaks for others and for injustice. She is a giver who is always thinking of someone else. Unlike my dad, she likes the gray area. The gray area accepts people and doesn't judge. My mom has a heart for babies and all kids, but newborns are her favorite. She has been the young woman who went from her parent's home to my dad's, and has been taken care of. I have watched her change into a more independent woman, a broken-hearted woman in these past few years, but she continues to persevere and make a difference in the lives of others. She serves in the orphanages in Guatemala, she makes shoe boxes for operation Christmas child, she feeds the homeless and positions her life towards the service and plight of those without a voice.

I've been positioned by the legacies of my parents and the gifts that God has given me. I'm the little blonde teacher in charge of the English learners and newcomers from Mexico due to my love of culture and language from my childhood in Panama. I was a kindergartener in Panama who on the first day of school, got on a multi-colored school bus with a driver that had gold teeth and a warm smile. I learned Spanish in elementary school. I was the minority. I like to make everyone feel important and worthy. I like to have a good time; I am very social. As far as faith is concerned, I absolutely have convictions of what I believe to be true. With that, I have a more gentle side that has no room for the judgment of others. The traits of both of my parents have been passed down and the unique combinations make me the person I am today.

My sisters Kristi and Katie also carry the threads of both of my parents. My sister Kristi is dependable and practical. She has the heart and bed-side manner of a nurse and I know that I can count on her. Her three kids, Jake, Monica, and Shelby as well as her husband John, have added immensely to my life and my loss. They loved Emma to pieces and she loved them. Emma would call her cousins one name, "Jakmoncasheby" in a squeaky voice. She would pretend to talk to John on the phone and she loved John's cycle (motorcycle). My three kids and Kristi's three kids always paired up. It was just very natural. Tyler would hang with Jake; Shelby and Jayden are two of a kind; and Monica loved her partner Emma. Monica has always been a little mommy, but she and Emma shared something special.

And then there is my little sister Katie, who is 15 years younger than me. I might say that she spent as much time with Emma as I did. I'm pretty sure that she loved her as much. The plan for the upcoming school year was that Katie was going to come to my house and watch Emma everyday while I was at work. I grieve because that never happened. Emma used to call her "T" and her husband Chris "Tis". Katie and Chris also had a little dog Roxy, who Emma loved.

Emma would call her "Saucy". The year before, Katie watched Emma at our house every Friday. Emma would love the attention and the "girl time". Katie would paint her fingers and toes, bring her donuts, take her to the park, and I always knew that when I got home, Emma would have a new hairdo! Katie spent every day following Emma's passing at my house, cleaning, folding laundry and doing anything I needed. Her heart is broken as all of ours is. Katie got a beautiful tattoo on her arm that has a picture of the purple bow Emma was wearing "that night" with an "E" in the center; it says, "A dream is a wish your heart makes." Following Emma's death Katie would share dreams that she would have of Emma. The dreams inspired the tattoo. They had a very special bond and I'm not sure why Katie has been burdened with such a load of grief at such a young age. She has however, had the ability to continually encourage me throughout my stages of grief. Katie would write lyrics to me with a note, such as "I'm sorry that you have to be the mother who's not even grey but buries her baby."

My family and Matt's family have all been hurt by the loss of Emma. Matt's family has felt the void of Emma especially during the holidays when we gather. There are four grandsons on the Vargas side and Emma was the only granddaughter. She caught everyone's eye and she captured their hearts.

So as I write this book, my thoughts have been acquired by my life's experiences and my relationship with God aside from my parents, but their influence has laid the foundation which all has been built upon. I have lost a lot. The bruises that are left are ever-present. The blessings in my life have left their marks as well...and the largest mark has been a wonderful family who raised me with the love of Christ at the center.

Our Little "Amazing Grace"

When it comes to our children, we all have a story to tell. We all think our children are the cutest, the smartest, and just the most wonderful people we have ever seen. I am not going to attempt to state that Emma was more extraordinary than other two year olds, than your two year old. What I hope to do is share her life with you. If you didn't have the opportunity to know her, hopefully through these words you will get the sense of the impact her short life has made on others, and perhaps inspire all of us.

As a baby, Emma was so easy. She was content and liked everyone. The activity of the boys or her daycare never really affected her. She was just a go with the flow kind a girl. She was very petite and mellow. Her nursery was complete with pink and green and paintings that were of wild grasses that the boys had painted for her. Two sayings were on the walls in her room: A wee bit of heaven drifted down from above (which is now on her headstone) and BLOOM (the title of this book). It's as if the sayings were prophetic. Although she had a beautiful nursery, she was so little and easy, that Matt liked her sleeping in our room in her bassinet. She slept through the night at two months old and she was a snug lil bug beside us. That is not unusual, except for one morning when she was about 9 months old, she sat up out of her bassinet and waved at us! We cracked up laughing, "Ok, if you can sit up and wave, you're too big to be in this bassinet!" She was never opposed to sleeping in her crib, so from that moment on, she slept in her crib.

When it was time for me to go back to work, Emma would go to Miss Ronda's childcare center. (Miss Ronda had also cared for her brothers until they went to kindergarten.) The other kids there, Colie, Caleb, and Bella loved her and even named all of their baby dolls "Emma Grace". Miss Ronda had a nickname for all of the kids (Colie is actually

Nicole) and Emma would be known as "Gracie Goosie". These names were endearing and born out of love. We all started calling her Gracie, Goosie, Emmy, and so many other names. She fit in perfectly even though she was just a baby. Miss Ronda says that she had an ability to bring everyone together even at that young of an age.

When I was pregnant, my mom bought me a handmade sling from Guatemala. People got used to seeing me with the sling and nothing more than a bow or flower sticking out of it. Emma was completely content in there, and again due to her petite size, I carried her in that thing until she was about 10 months old.

During this same time, Emma was on the move. Because she was our third child, I didn't feel the need to buy a playpen or any of the other "baby extras". Once she became mobile she was in to everything. So Matt, being the fun dad that he is, bought a giant blow-up pool and put it in the center of our living room! He filled it with her blankets and toys. She couldn't get out of it and she had about nine feet of playing area in the large circle. She was happy, and we were happy because she was contained and it cost only ten dollars!

After Emma turned one, she was still easy-going but had a desire to be a "big girl" and now she began to play side by side with the older kids at the preschool. Often she was the first one to arrive at preschool and she would set everyone's plates and cups. She loved rocking and hushing baby dolls. She loved cooking in the kitchen, and did so many girl things that were new to me. She had an ability to draw people to her. The other kids liked playing with her because there were no conditions, just simple joys.

As she was growing that year, a little personality was emerging. She was very verbal at a young age. If you asked her how to spell her name, she would say in her squeaky little voice 'E-M-M-A. We all thought she was brilliant! She wasn't event two! Emma knew what language that we did not find acceptable, like "shut-up". She began to say "shubup" when we told her anything she didn't want to hear. When she learned that that came with consequences, she learned how to squeak it without opening her mouth…so that we couldn't really get her in trouble for it. She had this awesome balance of spunk met with ease. (Mommy's girl indeed)

After a celebration at the preschool one day, I noticed a rash when I gave her a bath that night. We narrowed it down to a few candies (including grape Nerds). I didn't think much of it until the next time she ate Nerds and broke out again. Then I thought it was the purple dye. So, being the fearless mother that I am, I experimented on her with the other flavors of Nerds and other Willy Wonka candies to see if it was the purple dye. She didn't break out with a purple grape Runt or Gobstopper, (other Willy Wonka candies) and did break out with all of the other colored Nerds. To sum it up, she was *allergic to Nerds!* I couldn't wait to make her a shirt one day stating that fact!

Once Emma turned two, the Little Miss emerged. She had become a little girl. She could say everything. She was potty trained, and when I would do laundry and she would see her clothes, she would scream, "My panties!!!" She cleaned her room, played games, chose which boots she wanted to wear, and loved her hair bows and jewelry.

Emma loved reading books, and she had these realistic picture books that were her favorite. As she would point to each picture and say its name like, "nest", I would say "Yes". She learned to read that book and would say yes after each picture because she thought that was how it went… apple- yeeees; goat- yeeees; queen- yeeeees. She also had an emerging speech lisp like her brother Tyler. It is very paradoxical to hear smart, intelligent vocabulary with a lateral "s".

One night as I was lying in bed reading my bible, I desperately wanted quiet time. Emma crawled up next to me and said, "I read!" I said, "No, mommy's reading her bible right now." She said, "My bible" and off she went to her room to get her bible. I really wanted to read alone, but she cozied up next to me and opened her bible. With a sigh, I closed mine. I remember thinking, "Enjoy this moment for they are fleeting." I began to talk about the pictures with her and the characters. I said, "Who's that?" She would say, "A man." (It was Adam). We would do that with all of the bible characters and she began to recognize Jesus different than the other men of the bible. I would point and she would say "a man" or "Jesus". When we would see Jesus in the bible, I would begin singing "Jesus Loves the Little Children" to her. She would hush me and tell me to stop! I laughed and then she would laugh. I would do it even more to annoy her! She colored on sermon notes that day that I still have in my bible. This day comforts me in a weird way because I felt like she was "introduced" to Jesus. I know that's probably weird, but it's true.

Emma had this wonderful balance of being coordinated and athletic like her brothers, and she was all-girl in the next moment. She had an incredible sense of humor even at a young age. When she would smile, her big blue eyes disappeared, dimples on her cheeks surfaced, and her nose wrinkled. A scrunchy, smiley face became her trademark. Emma was a peace-maker who brought people together. She had a quiet spirit, but she was a leader. She had influence in her whisper and influence in her death. There are lessons to be learned from our little Grace, our "Amazing Grace" if we choose to reduce ourselves to the profound simplicity of a child.

Emma Grace...a large life!

The strength of a man- some words from Emma's dad

Like driftwood in the ocean,

I await the waves of God to gently guide me to land.

The morning rise and evening setting of the sun docs the time
as I await.

I know that I cannot reach shore any sooner than his current
will allow,

So I wait on him, adrift, but willing to be moved

Up, down, side to side, and then eventually forward.

Trusting Him I will get wet, but will not sink to the ocean
floor.

I will be wiped dry soon and I will stand

And then eventually walk, with his direction as my compass.

Matt Vargas
December 12, 2010

*Today is the first day of spring though all around us it is
overcast with clouds and rain*
*Just like spring flowers, we all need the Son to thrive, grow
and eventually bloom into the amazing wonder
that God has created us to be.*
*During our growth, we must weather many storms, cloudy
days, and at times blinding fog.*
*The sun during these times seems so far away, unseen with
our eyes, its warmth unfelt,*
Even though it is revolving around us at all times.
Today I encourage you to look up to God's Son.
*Know that he is there; absorb His light, His love, His
warmth.*
*I pray that today, the flower in the heart of your inner
garden Blooms!*

Matt Vargas
March 2011

Part 1- Suffering

"The righteous cry out, and the Lord hears, and delivers them out of all their troubles. The Lord is near to those who have a broken heart, and saves such as have a contrite spirit." Psalms 34

Heading for Home... July 6, 2010

Saying good-bye...

I'm still not really sure how one says good-bye to their child. When the world around observes such a thing, they are curious. They cannot fathom it. To tell you the truth, neither could I. The fact is, however, you do not have a choice when death comes to your door.

Matt and I chose to celebrate Emma's beautiful life. We chose not to wear black at her service. We so wanted to honor her life and the beginning of her legacy here on earth. The best thing we could do for her was to be strong and demonstrate the light that she was in our lives.

We were extremely fortunate to be surrounded by so many wonderful people who made her service beautiful. Countless friends and family rallied together and contributed to the day. We were amazed at the support and help everyone gave. It's not a day anyone wants to plan, but you are left with the choice to do one last thing for your loved one. I wanted to share her life with everyone. I didn't want the service to end.

The days following the service were quiet. Our house was quiet. Tyler said, "She brought life to our home, and now it is gone." I wasn't quite sure what to do with myself.

When you are used to the activity of a two-year-old, and then it is gone, you are left with emptiness. I bumbled around, so to speak, trying to fill my time and my arms.

I don't think we turned the T.V. on for two weeks. We couldn't take in one more thing. Our house was quiet. It was sad, but it was peaceful. We had lots of visitors and lots of tears. Everyone loved Emma and none of us wanted to say good-bye.

The boys and their friends carried on their usual activities because I didn't want to suddenly limit them from the things they loved. I let their desires be the compass in leading their grief. So we remained wrapped into the baseball all-star season.

To move in the days to come, we had to release her. We had to say good-bye. We had to accept that she will not be in our home anymore. She is with Jesus, and we will see her again, but never again would we see her here. The reality and finality of that is not easy, but acceptance proved to be a necessary step to move forward.

The Community Embraces Us

We live in the small community of Newman, California. This community has embraced our loss and has gone above and beyond in their support for us and our family.

From the very first day after losing Emma, the community was hard at work rallying together to organize a car wash, organize meals and countless random acts of kindness were done. Monetary donations were coming as well as flowers and well-wishes.

The baseball community had passed out pink ribbons for the kids and coaches to wear on their hats in her memory. Pink balloons were released after the game in her honor. Tyler had his second all-star game the very next night and he wanted to play. Matt took him and he played…in fact he was the first batter and hit a homerun! (The kind of homerun that shouldn't be a homerun- the ball just kept rolling and getting away from the Gustine team.) Everyone from both teams stood up and cheered. They were happy for Tyler, but it was as if it was for or from Emma. That was a game I couldn't go to…There was no way I could assume the same spot in the bleachers as the night before. The team including Matt and Tyler, released pink and white balloons into the summer sky. My sister Katie took pictures and as the balloons drifted up, Matt and Tyler's balloons kept coming back down; they hooked onto the fence before their final release. I know that is a memory that Matt and Tyler share and will never forget.

As the baseball season came to an end, Tyler's all-star team won 2nd place in the Newman Tournament and the coach gave the big team trophy to Tyler. I cried. Tyler asked, "Mom why are you crying? This is awesome!" This was the first game I had attended since. It was very hard, but I knew it was important to Tyler that I was there. I also knew that I was surrounded by people who loved me.

In the spring of 2011, the VonRenner Elementary School after-school program made a special tribute to Emma called, "The Emma Grace Garden Place". It is absolutely beautiful! The garden is such a touching and fitting memorial for her! There is a bench there for us to go and reflect. I love seeing her name. I think a fear of parents who lose a child is that people will forget. Seeing her name on such a big, beautiful mural reminds me that students will forever be playing outside and may ask, "Who is Emma?" And someone gets to share about her life.

The following year, as baseball season was nearing once again, I became terrified! How could I go to baseball practice or a game without my daughter? I was torn, sad, jealous, angry, and depressed. I had made up my mind not to attend opening ceremonies that year...until a friend and board member approached me. She wanted to know if it would be okay if the boys threw in the first pitch! I started sobbing. I said, "I wasn't even going to go!" She laughed. Of course I was going to be there to watch that honorable moment for them and for us. Our family has received several accolades and recognition. It's tough because on the one hand we are grateful for kind gestures, but we are quickly reminded that they were born out of our heartache. We are also very aware that not everyone who loses a child receives this type of condolence. I hope to be the hands and feet one day with the heart to give back. Every special act done for us has made the load of grief lighter...so thank you friends...thank you Newman!

The boys getting ready to throw in the first pitch!

The "Emma Grace Garden Place" at Von Renner Elementary School in Newman

The First Year

The beginning of the first year without Emma was uncharted territory for me. I had lost before. I have grieved before. But losing a child is a loss like no other grief in the world. Someone gave me a card that said, "When you lose your spouse, you are called a widow, when you lose your parents, you are called an orphan, but when you lose a child there are no words." That is so true. It is completely unexplainable.

Everything I did that first year was hard. Going to work was hard. Attending family functions was hard. Getting dressed was hard. The holidays were hard. Being at church was hard. Even waking up each day was hard. I wanted my easy-carefree life back.

I will touch on the specifics of going back to work and the holidays in another chapter, but the incredible weight of grief that is carried during the first year must be recognized. It consumed my mind, my heart, my emotions, and my speech. It was all that I could think about, and all that I could talk about.

I remember going to the dentist shortly after losing Emma. I sat in the chair at the dentist's office and I could hear people from the other rooms talking and laughing. I thought to myself, "How can people just keep talking? How can they be so carefree?" Tears streamed down my face. This was one of the first times that I had left my home, and the realization that life for everyone else had continued like normal. That's right; I was the only one that was different. As the hygienist came into my room, she noticed I was upset. She said in a sweet voice, "We can reschedule this; we really don't have to do this now." I snapped, "Do you think I'll be better in December? Because I won't be! This will not go away and I will not be healed! So just do what you have to do and I'll leave." This behavior was out of character for me.

This was the beginning of my grief-stricken life…and I didn't like it one bit.

During this time, I also unconsciously said good-bye to "Flashy Heather", and hello to a new "Modest Heather". I could no longer wear my trademark high heel shoes because I viewed them as "happy shoes". I couldn't wear bright clothes. I started wearing a lot of grey and navy. One day as I was shopping with my sister Katie, I had my arms full of clothes to try on, and she said, "Uh, that pile looks a little drab! It looks like you are carrying a cloud." And I said, "Well that is how I feel." This continued for the whole first year. I was giving away my pride, my confidence. How could I strut my stuff? I had nothing to strut. The only thing I could wear was a broken heart.

Some days I would find myself in a store or a restaurant, and I would think, "What am I doing here? I lost my daughter… I had a hard time putting myself in places that were considered "enjoyable" as if it were dishonoring Emma. Generous people had given us gift cards and gift certificates for places. I know the intent was for us to get out and do something with the boys. It did work because it forced us to do things that we probably would have not chosen to do. But as I would observe myself in those places, sitting in a theatre, at John's Incredible Pizza, or the waterslides, I felt like I was in a movie. I was observing everything, and I tried to just be present for the boys, but I would think, "How can I be laughing out loud at the movies when I just lost my daughter?!" I suppose looking back, it was good for me. I think it is good sometimes to force yourself to do what you don't "feel" like doing.

Before Emma's death, I had signed up for a three-day teachers' conference in Sacramento. It was scheduled for August, just one month after Emma's death. I made the decision to go to the conference because I was going to be teaching something new that year and I didn't know the program. At the time, everything felt like a grief blur. I didn't know what was "normal" and what wasn't. Going to a conference didn't seem any more absurd than making dinner for my family and setting only four places. Looking back, I wonder what I was thinking! I had no business being at a teacher's conference a month after losing my daughter!

The main character in the literature we studied was named Emma…Really?! I held it together and completed the conference. On the way home from Sacramento, I stopped into a Party City store to buy "soccer cut-outs" for my classroom. I was not at all prepared for what I was about to see: Halloween Costumes! They took my breath away. The first one I saw was Emma's exact costume from the year before…a ladybug. It was only August- I had not prepared my heart or my mind for Halloween yet.

Once school started, the mornings felt like an eternity. I was used to juggling three kids before school with one being a toddler. Now the boys got themselves ready and I only had to worry about myself. I didn't care that I now had time to make myself a "decent lunch". In the past, I would drop the boys off at my in-laws' house where Tom (my father in-law) would be waiting outside each morning to be greeted by Emma. She would wave and yell "Papa!" His morning greetings would never be the same either. Now I had one less stop at daycare so I found myself ready an hour early every day. When you find time under circumstances like mine, you can't just fill it with exercise or cleaning. I would go back home and just cry; I suppose I squeezed in more grief time. One day I wrote in my journal:

Change is hard. Today marks three months.
I cut my hair and we are making lots of changes at home.
I'm struggling between holding on and moving forward.
I'm not settled.
I had looked forward to Emma and me getting matching bob haircuts.
Last night, I went to the salon alone.
For a fresh start; not a good start.
As a marking of sorts representing change, loss, sadness.

I walked into the house last night sad.
I'm changed. My family has changed. My home is changing.
It seems like the rest of the world is staying the same.
I'm beginning to wonder if people are getting tired of me
talking about my feelings.
October 6, 2010

The first cold, dark autumn day was upon us. I stayed home and sobbed the whole day. I didn't like the weather changing. It represented leaving the season when I had Emma. The cold wind represented time passing. I knew it was the beginning of entering a season, many seasons without Emma.

Gray Day
Seasons, Halloween, Change
Happy families, Costumes, treats
Sadness, Sorrow, Envy

Desire, Progress, Painting
Moving, Needing, Hoping
Bright Day on the Horizon
November 1, 2010

My sister Katie came over to help me sort through some of Emma's things. Months before Emma died, Matt had been working to turn a family room into an additional bedroom for Tyler so that the boys could have their own rooms. Since after her passing, we were already involved in the changes of a remodel, this caused us to have to make decisions about her room and her things quicker than we would have otherwise made them. So we talked with Tyler. We made decisions about the rooms. This involved us "taking down" Emma's room. Katie came to help me sort through her things into piles- keep, donate, give to…etc. This was *a horrible, horrible* day. I held onto her things, I smelled them. Her scent was still on everything. I kept special things and clothes. Katie kept some too. Then we began to make piles. Nice things, clothes with tags…and older clothes and things. We decided to take some of the nicer things and furniture to a well known second hand chain store. I called ahead to let them know I was coming with a car full of things and to warn them of the situation. I said, "I do not want to be haggled; I do not care about money; I just need a place to go." The woman assured me that it would be ok. We loaded my car top to bottom and Katie even had to hold things on her lap. Once we arrived, Katie unloaded lamps, changing pads, strollers, bags of clothes, etc. out of my car. Once in the store, the lady asked us to leave our things and they would call us once they have gone through everything. This was perfect as I could not bear to watch them hold Emma's things up for evaluation! Katie and I ran into a Target store across the street. We were not even in the store for 10 minutes when we got a call. We were surprised how quick they were, so we left Target and went back across the street. We weren't sure what to expect, however we never expected what was about to happen. As we entered the store with already sick stomachs, a lady said, "All we can use is the step stool and a toy." What? It took every bit of emotional and physical strength to even load the car and make the trip to begin with. I said, "What? Didn't you assure me this would not happen?" A very rude lady said, "Oh, well I am not going to go through all of your dirty clothes." Katie and I were fighting back tears. Dirty clothes? Did she really say dirty clothes? I ferociously started pulling clothes out of the bag with tags on them…brand new clothes…I said what do you mean dirty clothes? She said, "Oh, well if you want to go through the bag and pull out clothes with tags, we'll take a look at those." Katie and I were furious! We said forget it and took all of our things back home! I would rather give everything to needy families who could use them than to support this horrible business. There were no dirty or stained clothes in that bag. I knew a business wouldn't want those. I had already selected only the best, and not to be snotty but Emma's things were very nice and everything was like new. Emma just had her 2nd birthday and many of her brand new things were in the bags. We ended up giving things to different people who could use them…probably what I should've done to begin with. I just wanted a thoughtless, one stop, let's get this over with kind of day. Instead it added insult to injury. I still cannot believe how rude and insensitive they were. I will never step foot into that store again! I kept my favorite newborn outfits, baby outfits, and toddler outfits. They are labeled in tubs in her special closet. I kept all things that reminded me of her and things to help me to feel close to her. She has tubs labeled "bows and shoes", "blankets and bb's" and so on. Even with all that I kept, there was still much more that just didn't make sense to keep. A friend of mine Maggie Keddy, asked me for some of Emma's clothes so she could make a quilt with some of her outfits. I agreed and it is beautiful! It is a wonderful way to do something with the clothes rather than just tuck them away. As we slowly "took down" Emma's room, we began to gather and build up a special space for her memory…a space that in fact, Emma herself hammered nails into- A space for her to forever shine in our house.

Emma's closet where I keep her things…All things, her favorite books, movies, baby dolls, blankets and even her "prize box" for going potty (which still has tic-tacs in it). The picture on the right is the quilt made out of Emma's clothes. Each flower on the quilt was a dress or a shirt that reminds me of her. I love it! Thank you Maggie!

Thanksgiving was hard. What did I have to be thankful for? I didn't want to visit with family and show up the same as I did every previous year. Again, everyone else's lives were the same, and I felt like the outcast. If I didn't have other children, I probably would have chosen to just forget the holidays altogether. But when you have kids counting on you to "show up" emotionally, it would've been harder to explain to them why we were not doing anything than to just go. I definitely was thankful for them.

Feeling strength today, some energy.
I feel like God is giving me peace about the future.
It will be okay.

"You can gain strength, courage and confidence by every experience in which you really stop to look fear in the face. You must do the thing you think you cannot do"
Eleanor Roosevelt

Christmas was upon us and I desperately wanted to be celebrating this with all my kiddos. I wanted to hang three stockings. I wanted to shop for three kids. The magic of Christmas was gone. The boys' interests and gifts were boring to me; Xbox 360, iPods and footballs. Older kids' gifts didn't feel the same as a baby doll or a rocking horse. I knew that they still deserved their Christmas and that those gifts wouldn't bother me if I had Emma, so it wasn't about them or their gifts. It was about me. We celebrated Christmas and gave ourselves over to the boys. It did bring me enjoyment watching them. They did make me happy, at least for awhile.

*　　　*　　　*

The New Year hit me like a ton of bricks. I did not want the calendar to change. I did not want to leave the last year with Emma. Time was moving forward and I wanted it to go back. If one more person said "Happy New Year" to me I was going to punch them in the face. The year before, we threw a New Year's party where the kids played bingo and Emma wore a hat and blew her horn. I wanted another New Year like that one. Matt's sister Dianne and her husband Randy gave the boys a trip to Disneyland for Christmas.

They were going to take them during the week of the New Year's celebrations. I was happy for the boys, and knew that I had no business being at the "happiest place on earth". When Dianne and Randy came to pick up the boys, they were so excited! As they drove away, I went into the house and cried. This was another example of how my life had changed. Before, I would've never let someone else take my kids to Disneyland without me. This time turned out to be a blessing, a time to come off of the holidays and just grieve. Matt and I would just lie around, we watched football, and I even popped open a bottle of wine. New year's Resolutions indeed. What did this New Year, this future hold for me?

*   *   *

Time did pass. I probably read at least 20 books on grief. I wanted to do this grief thing right. The information on grief was hard for me because it is all about how there is no "right way." I'm good at following directions, so I wanted a book that said, "Do X, Y, Z and then you'll be better." I learned that it was not that easy. So I continued down the road, the long, winding, unpredictable road of grief.

*   *   *

February was here. It had been seven months without my sweet Emma. I was planning Jayden's 7th birthday. He was going to have a disco dance party! I found myself in Party City buying disco balls, strobe lights, gangsta hats and the like. I was having a woman who worked there blow up some "record shaped" balloons. She began to inquire about my party…and then the questions. How many kids do you have? Boys or girls? With a deep breath, I gave it to her. She said, "Well you are cute and sweet. How come you look cute and sweet?" I answered, "Because my son is turning seven." I said, "My son is entitled to a fun party. Don't get me wrong, I am very aware of where the 'girls garden party' section is that I bought for my daughter nine months ago. I just can't go there. Today my son is turning seven, and today I am buying supplies for his birthday." She cried and hugged me. So even the joyous moments were hard.

*   *   *

Spring, baseball, and Easter were more of the same. I had begun to accept this life. I was also saving my emotional strength for the roller coaster in May to come: Tyler's birthday, Emma's birthday, my birthday, and Mother's Day. Baseball games, wrapping up work, and balancing my grief caused me to take action! So to take care of all of the stress in my life, I dyed my platinum blonde hair brown, well reddish actually. That's right, that and some new make-up would make all my problems go away. Some women change their hair color with their outfits, but not me. I've been a blonde my whole life. I remember when my mom saw it for the first time. I think she was fighting back tears. It's not that she didn't like it; it just didn't look like "me".

*   *   *

For Tyler's 10th birthday, he had a "sports" party which included 12 boys playing a baseball game, football game, soccer game, basketball and swimming. It was fun! Emma's birthday and mine would be spent on a cruise escaping the reality of the days. Mother's Day was a surprise to me. I had anticipated hard days, but completely underestimated Mother's Day. The boys were offering smiles and gifts and all I could do was cry the entire day. I explained to them that when you are a mom, it is hard to celebrate Mother's Day without all of your kids. They understood and I tried to receive their love.

The first Mother's Day…How do I celebrate without all of my babies? But how do I not accept the undeniable love from the boys, wholly as if they were (are) enough?! I found myself in a black velour sweat suit, I have dark hair, and I am a different mom from last year. I want all of my babies. We go to the cemetery early Sunday morning to "unite" as close as we can as a family. I can't bear to go to church for fear of someone saying, "Happy Mother's Day"... It's not happy at all. As I am sitting at Emma's grave crying, Jayden is rubbing my head and my back. I am crying. He says, "Mom, the top of your head feels like Keisha (our dog)". I laugh amidst my tears and I am thankful once again for my boys who know just how and when to snap me out of my misery. Mother's Day 2011

Emma's birthday also brought up emotions that I didn't expect, like reflecting on the day she was born, bringing her into the world, and now she is not here. I felt like when she was born, I was in charge of protecting her, and I failed. Nope, my reddish-brown hair didn't fix anything. More lessons learned about grief and myself.

* * *

Summer was here. I pushed through working an entire school year and I did it! I was proud of myself for not giving up. I was happy that I could spend a few months releasing more grief and spend some time to just be with myself. I did that. It was the lowest point on record. I was officially depressed. No one or nothing could make me happy. I didn't want anything and I didn't want to go anywhere. I gave myself the whole summer to really just "feel".

* * *

June brought Father's Day, another really tough day, as I had captured some precious photos the year before of Matt and the kids. And then our 15th anniversary. Our anniversary had been celebrated with a family beach trip the year before.

This year, Matt and I went to the beach alone to reflect. We needed to make peace with that place. Again, we felt like we were watching other people live; other families without a care in the world. Just days after those dates were the Fourth of July, and then finally the anniversary of Emma's death.

*   *   *

The Fourth was approaching and the boys were getting excited about fireworks. I didn't really want to have anything to do with fireworks as I could remember the year before capturing a picture of Matt and Emma gazing up into the night's sky. Tyler was not happy with me. He and Jayden had said that they would buy fireworks with their own money. I snapped. "You guys, this is not about money. I've put your feelings before my own and put myself in uncomfortable situations all year, and I'm asking for the 4th and the 6th, Can you give me that?" They understood, but still felt like they were suffering an injustice. They also didn't understand why I wouldn't go to the parade as we had done every year since they were born. I couldn't imagine sitting at the parade and seeing everyone. We didn't go. We did host a barbeque with swimming; a low-key family day. I let them go to their friend's houses to watch fireworks at night. I just wanted that day and the rest of the week to sail by me.

*   *   *

On the anniversary of Emma's death, July 6th, Tyler had an all-star game just like the year before. Really? Was I really going to place myself at a baseball game wearing purple on that day? I gave myself options out, but ended up going to the game. I just focused on Tyler. Family and friends surrounded us. We left the game and all went to the cemetery together. I played my "Heather missin' Emma playlist". We all sat around a circle and offered hugs and memories. Matt went home after the game, because he tends to be more private in his grief. I had learned that we all grieve differently and everyone's styles need to be respected. I sent out this text to family and friends:

Today I am choosing to celebrate Emma's 1ˢᵗ anniversary in heaven. She has been made perfect and is more beautiful there than she ever was here. As for me, I am thankful that this is the last "first" I will have to experience. We have gotten through this past year with the help of friends, family, and God's righteous right hand that continues to hold us. Love you all, Heather

We did get through all of those dates as difficult as they were. I kind of felt a sense of relief on July 7ᵗʰ, because I had experienced all of the firsts. No more anticipation and uncharted territory. This road had become paved. I knew this road. I still preferred the smooth, fast highway, but the bumpy country road of my grief had become the new road. As I began to accept my new road, life began to get easier. I've realized that I have control of my choices and who I want to be. I've also realized that staying on the bumpy road is a choice.

*   *   *

Entering the second year without Emma was inevitable, so I chose to merge back onto the highway. I am choosing to live life large to honor Emma. The best thing I can do in her memory is to shine my light, just as she did here on earth.

If I could set this book to music, I would. Music aided in my healing more than any other one thing. I listened to this playlist every morning for the first year. I took it to the cemetery with me. I cried. I praised. I surrendered. I loved. I was filled. And eventually the music changed. The second year, I created a Heather praisin' playlist and the songs became more upbeat. Today I alternate between those playlists and Heather's mix each morning; a mix of genres which includes the good, the bad, and the ugly... evidence perhaps that the season has changed. I still love all of these songs, and if you are suffering, I encourage you to check them out!

Heather Missin' Emma Playlist

Homesick- Mercy Me
Strong Enough- Matthew West
Before the Morning- Josh Wilson
Bring the Rain- Mercy Me
I Can Only Imagine- Mercy Me
Cry Out to Jesus- Third Day
Heaven is the Face- Steven Curtis Chapman
Blessed Assurance- Chris McClarney
Come to Me- Jadon Lavik
Glorious day- Casting Crowns
All of Me- Matt Hammitt
The Redeemer- Sanctus Real
Hope Now- Addison Road
I Will- Justin Fox
If I Die Young- The Band Perry
You Can Have Me- Sidewalk Prophets
Hear Our Song- Jadon Lavik
Family Tree- Matthew West
White Horse- Taylor Swift
Strong Enough to Save- Tenth Avenue North
Save a Place for Me- Matthew West
In Better Hands- Natalie Grant
Starry Night- Chris August

Spring Is Coming- Steven Curtis Chapman
Today is Your Day- Shania Twain
Walk By Faith- Jeremy Camp
I Still Believe- Jeremy Camp
Wish You Were Here- Mark Harris
Held- Natalie Grant
Bring It all together- Natalie Grant
Amazing Grace- Chris Tomlin
By Your Side- Tenth Avenue North
Where I Belong- Building 429
Love Has Come- Mark Schulz
Paintings in my Mind- Tommy Page
Blessings- Laura Story
All Who Are Thirsty- Kutless
Wish You Were Here- Lady Gaga
He is with you- Mandisa
If We've Ever Needed You- Casting Crowns
Lead Me- Sanctus Real
Anyway- Martina McBride

Grieving and Raising Kids

I now know that from minutes after losing Emma I had a job to do. My job was to offer structure and stability for the boys. I was determined to make sure that they wouldn't be crazy. I had lost one child; I wasn't about to lose my other two to insanity.

More than willpower, I am recognizing this period as shock. It is common when someone feels they have a "job to do" after loss for their state of shock to be prolonged until they feel their job is done. So we carried on as a family and did normal activities. Neighbor kids came over to visit. The first day they came over after our loss, they were holding a bucket of chicken with their heads hanging low. I talked with them, I assured them that it was okay for them to come and play and, in fact, my boys needed them to. Matt and I had to prepare ourselves emotionally for the activity of the boys and their friends. For two weeks after Emma passed, he and I would sit by the pool with our coffee every morning before the boys would wake up. We had to make peace out there. We couldn't let the pool represent all that Emma was. I chose to remember the fun times in the pool with Emma- she loved it. Each morning that Matt and I were out there, the sun was shining, the birds were singing…we had to choose to create peace in our surroundings. If your loved one died in a car accident, would you never get into a car again? I chose to think in those terms. We knew that the boys and their friends would be asking to swim again soon. It was July. So, I told all the kids that our house was not weird and the pool was not off limits. I told them that they may see me cry from time to time; but that they don't need to be nervous around me…it was just me missing Emma. They understood because they missed her too! Some would even say when they knocked on the door and I answered, "Oh, I'm used to Emma coming to the door with you, sigh."

I never wanted the boys to grow up and say, "After my sister died, we could never play baseball or swim again." To me that would not be fair to them. So they continued to do all of their usual activities.

The boys reacted very differently from one another in their grief due to their ages and personalities. Jayden would say things matter of fact daily. Like, "Don't you think 20 is the earliest someone should die Mom? Don't you think 20? Not 2?" I'd say, "Yes, Jayden, that sounds reasonable to me." Then he would say, "Mom don't you notice everyone else has a baby with a stroller? We used to, but we don't anymore." With a giant sigh and a heavy heart I would say, "Yes Jayden." We had conversations like that daily. He was processing and grieving. One night as I was tucking Jayden in for bed he said, "Mom you know what's weird? When Emma was here, we taught her everything, but right now she knows more than us." He said, "When we die and go to heaven, she will teach us and show us around." I smiled and cried. It was what I needed to hear. As a mom, I never felt like she would teach me, but Jayden understood and taught me how once we die all will be revealed. It's pretty amazing because that was not information he heard an adult say, in fact it never occurred to any of us.

Tyler summed it up by saying, "Emma was the light in our house and now it is gone." Most days Tyler was very cautious of what he said, so he didn't say much. In fact, he was angry. He was happiest playing with his friends, playing ball, or anything else to distract him from his life. One night as his anger was building, we had a long talk and I recognized its origin. He felt guilty. He felt like everyone would be happier if it were him instead. Once we addressed the issue, his anger and bitterness subsided. One day as I was crying, Tyler put his arm around me and said, "What's wrong?" I said that I was missing Emma. He said, "Mom, we all do. We wish she was here, but the best thing we can do is continue to live." I will say that I have pretty awesome kids! Kids that for some reason have a peace and true understanding about life and death that even us adults struggle with.

Parenting will never be as carefree as it was before. I always consider how a decision I make may affect them. It takes an enormous amount of emotional and mental strength and it is exhausting! I am so thankful for Tyler and Jayden. If it weren't for them, I could very possibly still be in bed! They gave me a purpose to do things that were hard. In the end, I benefited as well.

It was hard to strike the balance in parenting from grieving the loss of one child, to not allowing your other children to feel like she was more important than them. As we remodeled the game room, I was pulling out some pictures of Emma and our family, and Matt said, "You know this is their room to play, maybe we shouldn't display photos of Emma all over this room." I thought that was wise.

It is difficult to assist your children in grief when you are grieving yourself. It was only once I felt like they were going to be okay (around October of 2010) that my true grief actually began. At that point, I knew that they were secure. I knew that I could let my guard down and have hard days. In fact, not only could I, but I thought it necessary to model "real grief" for them.

This journey will continue for their lives and mine. As for today, they are two thriving kids who amaze us daily with the gifts that God has given them. I am thankful for today and I will just live one day at a time.

Brotherly Love

Some pictures Tyler and Jayden drew of our family after our loss. August 2010

Tyler drew it just as he remembered…and how he still wanted it.

Jayden said, "I would…I would…have put Emma but we can't hold her hand.

Irrational Thoughts; Irrational Moments

I like to think of myself as a very level-headed person whose decisions do not blow with the wind. That is mostly true, until I was grieving that is. Here is a list of times where I was irrational in the first year. If you are grieving, give yourself a break…You are not crazy! You are hurting. And if you are dealing with someone who is grieving, give them some grace! It is temporary, and I don't think anybody, no matter how sane they are, can avoid irrational moments during grief.

Because the night Emma died I was making homemade tacos (frying the shells), I could not bring myself to make that meal again. The problem is that it's one of the boys' favorite meals. I told them that it was hard for me and we could have tacos with hard shells. Tyler said, "C'mon mom! It's just a taco!" He was right. I eventually eased in to frying the shells again.

I would not go into our local grocery store, Nob Hill, for about two months. I am a "regular" and many of the employees grew to know and love Emma. I just didn't want to see them. I didn't want to walk with my cart without her in it. I also felt like people would stare at me. So I would send Tyler in the store with money to buy things. As he was in the store, I would cry. I would think, "What am I doing? You know he is going to come out with lettuce instead of cabbage! He is only nine after all." But I just couldn't do it.

We were upon Labor Day and Newman's fall festival. I didn't want to have any part of that. I stayed away. I remember telling Matt that the boys were getting older, and they probably didn't care about the parade anyhow. He reminded me that *actually* Jayden was only a first grader and it wasn't fair to cut him off from those things so early. We did abstain from the festivities that first year.

It was time for Tyler's first basketball game. I was terrified to walk into the gym without Emma. The year before I would bathe her, put her pajamas on, wrap her in a blanket and watch Ty's practices. The games were even more fun! This year I told Matt I didn't think I could go into the gym. He said, "Are you never going to a game again?" He reminded me that I would have to face the gym at some point. He was right.

On Halloween in 2010, I wouldn't "make the drive to Hilmar" as I did on so many other years. I knew I was going to be with my family who love us and were also grieving themselves for Emma, but I couldn't bring myself to getting into the car. So I stayed home. Due to the remodel, our house had concrete floors and a mess. Matt painted and I passed out candy…really? It was Halloween and we were painting Emma's old room. The emotions surged. The boys wanted to trick or treat around the block. I went out with them and I walked down the middle of the street and cried.

Even almost two years later, I won't wear A's team clothing. I am a fan of my boys and their teams, but the "cheerleader" in me is gone. Emma was dressed in A's clothing at every game and so was I, but it just doesn't feel right to me anymore. I also will never paint my toe-nails yellow or purple again.

Inconsistent with decisions we would normally make, we got Jayden a kitten and Tyler a hamster. These were definitely due to grief; I thought, "If this will bring smiles to your faces then okay!"

To sum it up, I basically decided that I didn't want to see "happy people". "No, I can't go there because people might be happy and that will irritate me." I felt like I couldn't understand how people could continue to have "light" conversations about nothing. Don't they know what is really important? I knew it was not fair of me to put those feelings on others, so I would be cautious in choosing where I would go and where I wouldn't go.

I suppose a lot of the emotions that come out while grieving are not so much irrational as much as they are actions due to a broken heart. I didn't like the person I was now. I liked the happier, easy-going Heather; Not the Heather that comes with conditions.

Looking back, I understand why I had to go through those times to heal. I am thankful for so many people in my life that let me be. They allowed me to be irrational and crazy all the while loving me and waiting for my restoration. Their hope in me and in my healing is priceless.

Distraction lightens the load

I've only learned of all of the distractions that have come into our lives the first year upon reflection. Some of our distractions during grief included:

1. Working
2. Ripping up floors/painting the house
3. Allowing Jayden to paint his room "Tennessee Orange"
4. Buying four pairs of boots
5. Buying a new bedroom set
6. Changing my hair color
7. Matt gets a new hobby- a street bike to be exact!

Subconsciously, we went from one thing to the next to keep busy. Moments of quiet were hard. Everyone kept talking to me about our "new normal" and I wasn't sure how to achieve that in our same space. It caused us to change things around.

I remember wanting to be at work a lot. I dreaded the weekends. The weekends meant I had to deal with my emotions. I had to be still. I was with my family that did not include Emma. I preferred to just go to work and keep busy.

I still recognize when I am doing something as a distraction to my grief. I think distractions are okay as long as we know that that is what we are doing. For me, ripping up the floors in our home was a huge distraction to Halloween the first year. It did seem to help. The sadness wasn't gone during those times, I was just temporarily focused on something other than Emma and my grief.

Distractions come in many forms for different people. It can be food, alcohol, shopping, working, and countless others. It is just basically the thing that keeps us busy and distracted from real life. Distractions come as a result of much more than grief. (Couponing is my latest distraction)

As is true with most aspects in life, a balance seems to be best. It is okay to be distracted to get you through tough moments, but it is also vital to be real and grieve. You have to feel. For people who choose to stay in the mode of distraction or denial, the grief will not go away; it will just be put off for another time.

Grief is hard work. It takes a physical, emotional, and mental toll on your whole body. I was inactive for a whole year because I simply did not have the strength to exercise, and at the time I didn't care that my body was deteriorating. After the first year, I realized that to be strong emotionally, I had to be strong physically.

I suppose our biggest distraction was taking a weekend cruise for Emma's birthday. I just had to get out of town. My hope was to celebrate her birthday by demonstrating love and moving on for the boys. It was a distraction all right! It was a party boat! We felt very far from Emma there, which was not what we wanted. Sometimes we can plan something with the best intentions, and it just doesn't play out like we had hoped. I was surrounded by young people partying, and I was reflecting on my daughter's life and death in a lounge chair. Really? What was I thinking? At least the boys had an awesome time.

I suspect that we all like to numb ourselves from the bruises of life. I won't even say you shouldn't. I would just suggest to everyone that they should try to be honest and real with themselves. Be aware of what you are doing and why you are doing it.

Life's Not Fair!!!

Why Me? Why Not Me? Who Am I?

*My flesh and my heart may fail, but God is the strength
of my heart and my portion forever. Psalm 73:26*
*Lord, you have assigned me my portion and my cup; you
have made my lot secure. Psalm 16:5*

The question of "why me?" produces a different
response from me depending on the day. I have certainly
asked the question and wished that this wasn't my fate.
Especially on days when I am feeling sorry for myself, I
wonder why I have to be going through this. When I'm out
and I see families with their children intact, I wonder why I
don't have mine. I think it is human to stack yourself up
against someone else and when you feel someone else has
something you want, we shout, "That's not fair!!!"

I also have another perspective which I try to remind
myself of often. Is it fair that someone dies of cancer? Is it
fair that a child is abandoned? Is it fair that during natural
disasters someone may lose their spouse, their children, and
their home? Is it fair that someone is raised in a hostile home
where they are not loved? Is it fair that there are children
today starving somewhere? Talk about fair! Is it fair that
someone can't have children to begin with? I can go on and
on. To find peace one must ultimately accept their
portion...the good parts and the bad.

As I was recently helping a student with his presidents
report on Abraham Lincoln, I began reading his biography. I
learned that Abraham Lincoln had four sons. Three of the
four sons died very young leaving Abraham and his wife
with only one living son. Soon after, Abraham Lincoln was
assassinated. This family of six became a family of two in
just a few years. His widow probably cried, "Life's not fair."

She was eventually committed to an insane asylum by her son. I'm sure that is not the fate she saw coming as the wife of the President.

As loss finds its way into our lives, I find it interesting how we feel like we are the first ones to ever experience these things. We are not. Suffering has taken place throughout history. So, Why me? Why not me? Who am I really?

At one point or another, we will all suffer. Our suffering, our portions are different, but suffering is the same. Whether grief comes as a result of illness, disease or accidents, it is suffering. Family dysfunction, abuse and neglect are forms of suffering. Alcohol, drug, and sexual abuse are forms of suffering. Poverty, hunger, and the homeless are forms of suffering. Not everyone will suffer in the way that I have, but everyone will experience pain that causes us to shout, "Why me?" My hope is that as you forge through your valley, you are able to gain strength and peace, and one day stand on the mountain top.

Once I take a world view, I am humbled. I start thanking God for the blessings in my life. It goes something like this...Thank you God that we have our needs met. Thank you God that we have enough food and a cozy home to live in; Thank you for my boys, and for my husband. Thank you for blessing me with wonderful parents. Thank you for our health. I think in America we feel very entitled to a perfect life. When that does not happen, in any capacity, we Americans get depressed.

In much of the world, if a person had one full meal a day, they would be considered rich. We know of these stories. We see pictures of starving kids on TV. We feel bad, but then we turn the channel and our life resumes quickly.

Who am I that I think I should be spared from heartache? Am I really entitled to a perfect life? Why? Is that promised to any of us? No. The happy ending that most of us long for is not promised in this lifetime.

Someone might think these are extreme comparisons, and perhaps they are. They do offer a perspective, a world view that reminds us that we have a lot to be thankful for. If I only looked in my neighborhood, I would be depressed too. I need to expand the lenses I'm looking through, and perhaps so do you.

Part 2- Faith

What is faith? It is the confident assurance that what we hope for is going to happen. It is the evidence of things we cannot yet see.

Hebrews 11:2

Faith is personal. I did not turn to faith after losing Emma. It is not a crutch. I had it before the hardships came into my life. However and whenever faith intertwines with our inner beings, it is a personal experience. I am hoping to be sensitive in my writings on this topic while remaining true to my personal beliefs. I have chosen to include faith in my writings because when people ask me (as they often do) how I do it, I cannot separate my strength from my faith. My hope for all who read this is for them to ponder their own beliefs and perhaps be inspired to deepen their own faiths.

God Prepares Us- His Undeniable Presence

Reflecting on the events leading up to losing Emma, we have been able to identify circumstances that we believe God used to both prepare us and sustain us.

Most notably, the losses and "grief work" I had to experience before losing Emma prepared me for the big one. My response and my reaction to loss and losing a child would have been completely different if I didn't have some "experience" on this road.

I recall having conversations with friends a year before Emma died. In three different situations with different people, the subject of losing a child came up. My friends talked of it with horror and fear in their eyes. In all three cases, I remember being very calm, and these were my words, "I shouldn't speak about it because I haven't been there, but I honestly believe that if it happened to me, I would have peace and I would know that God was in control." Looking back I think that it was the Holy Spirit conditioning my heart and my mind.

About a month before Emma died, Matt began to tell me of some fears and feelings he would get regarding Emma. He said he was worried that something "bad" would happen. My responses were usually reactive and I would say something like, "Stop thinking bad thoughts; don't you know that God will protect us and our family?" He just couldn't shake those feelings. Twice he even ran outside and broke the screen to the backdoor because he heard something. Each time as he would come back into the house to find Emma and me playing, he would go to bed with an unsettled spirit. Matt tends to be pessimistic and doesn't always handle "little problems" well. We believe that God was preparing his mind and his heart for this big thing. This information would be questionable for me as well, except he shared it with me each time.

One day in particular, we were driving to Turlock and he began to share with me that his fears and feelings were becoming more realistic. I sighed and looked in the backseat at our three kids, and I remember smiling at Emma. She grinned back. I can remember that moment like it was yesterday.

Leading up to the week before losing Emma, Matt got a hold of Tyler's iPod. Tyler and I love Christian bands and concerts. Matt likes it, but he can take it or leave it, and he doesn't know much about the artists. One night he randomly selected Jeremy Camp's "I Still Believe" song. At the time, Matt was struggling with something at work, and his thoughts of something bad happening to Emma were consuming him. He sat on the couch and replayed that song over and over for about three hours. The lyrics expressed how he was feeling- "Scattered words and empty thoughts seem to pour from my heart; I've never been so torn before, Seems I don't know where to start..." Being the "supportive" wife that I am, I thought, "Well isn't this a great lil' hobby for you!" Unfortunately this was more than a hobby. Matt ended up using that song and the lyrics as his message at Emma's service.

If you don't think I'm weird yet, just hold on. As we were driving to Emma's memorial service on the way to Turlock, the radio was playing. As we approached the very spot where weeks before he had told me of his fears, the song "I Still Believe" began playing. We are confident that these were not all random coincidences, but rather that they were orchestrated.

I also recall being adamant that my niece Shelby couldn't stay the night on the 6th. This was strange because my sister Kristi and I always swapped our kids for our anniversaries because they are only two weeks apart. Her anniversary is on the 6th. I said to her, "I can keep her on the 5th, but not the 6th. I didn't have a particularly good reason why, I just knew I couldn't. I now feel that she wasn't "supposed to be there". If she were there, things probably would've been different because she and her sister Monica mothered Emma and followed her everywhere. Things were not supposed to be different as much as I would've liked them to be.

I remember purchasing a book when Matt and I decided to begin a family. It was called, "Emma and Mommy Talk to God". I don't remember where I got it or why I bought it, but I've kept it through moves and babies. When Matt and I contemplated girl names when we were having the boys, Emma was never on the list. Still I kept the book with the kids' libraries. The book resurfaced when Emma was about one. Tyler found it and he would read it to her often. Although I thought it was cute, I didn't pay it much attention. The book eventually found itself in a basket in Emma's room. When I went through her things in her room after she died, I picked up the book and began to read it. As I opened the book I noticed a little blonde girl in pink silky pajamas standing on her bed. The girl was stretching her arms up to three angels above her bed. It looked just like Emma, even down to the pajamas. The story is about how Emma's mom had taught her that we do not need to be afraid because Jesus loves us and that we are surrounded by special angels. After finding the book, I knew that I had kept it for all of these years for this moment. It was a gift from above. It gave me peace because as the girl looked and reached towards the angels in the story, she was so happy. Her face was one of pure joy, and I like to think that my Emma shared a moment just like that one.

Countless times since the loss of Emma, I have walked into the backyard distraught only to find white feathers in the pool in the place we found Emma. We have never had white feathers there before and it is not a spot where debris gathers. The skimmers are on the other side of the pool. I don't see white feathers there every day, but I do see them when I really need them. They are there when I am sad. They are there on "special days" and on days when I need to be reminded that everything is ok.

Feathers were present everyday for weeks following Emma's death. I knew they meant something but I was trying not to read too much into it. As weeks became months, I found myself peeking outside from time to time looking for them. Usually when I looked, they were there.

On Emma's (3rd) birthday, as we found ourselves escaping the reality of our lives on a cruise, Matt and I were alone. The boys were at the Fun Camp, and we went to the bow of the ship to soak up some rays. We could hardly enjoy our fancy cocktails. It was a beautiful day at sea. The scenery was difficult to appreciate because my insides were sick. I looked up and over my giant drink, and I saw a white drifting feather floating back and forth. I dropped everything, not caring how I looked to others, and ran to the edge of the ship. My eyes followed that feather up, down, around and it eventually disappeared. Even in the middle of the ocean, off of the coast of Mexico, a white feather found me.

One afternoon, I was especially sad. I walked outside and noticed there were no feathers. I plopped on a lounge chair and put my head in my lap. Minutes later, I lifted my head to find several white feathers. I said out loud, "Okay, I don't know what this is God if this is you, or angels who are comforting me, or a neighbor kid throwing feathers over the fence...whoever it is, don't stop because I still need it!" The anniversary of Emma's death marked the day with the most feathers. Listen, I'm "with it" enough to not create a crazy story that will make me appear looney. I am only sharing it because it is true. One awesome thing about God is that He knows us. He knows what comforts us all differently. He knew that Matt's preparation needed to be before to ease him into it, where I needed reminders from heaven afterward, that my daughter and my life were in His hands and that I needed to continue to trust Him.

One day I became curious of these white feathers so I did a little research. It is said that angels often use little white feathers as a symbol to draw your attention to them. As I kept reading, it read that if you ever see a cluster of white feathers or if there are several in a line, then the angels are around you in force. Fascinating! I have continued to look for these little gems, but they have not appeared in over eight months…not even on special days. Although I *want* them, I suppose I no longer *need* them.

There have been other little stories of comfort that we feel have unexplainable connections. I am not claiming to fully understand the supernatural world, but I *am* claiming to know that God's presence and His preparation in our lives has been undeniable.

Why do bad things happen to good people?

Matt says, "Bad things don't happen to good people, bad things happen to all people." Ultimately that is true. There are no patterns to follow to find heartache or tragedy. It happens to the best of us and to the worst of us.

Ecclesiastes 9:2 says, *All things come alike to all: One event happens to the righteous and the wicked; to the good, the clean, and the unclean.*

I suppose as a society we feel like life should be fair, and when it is not, we don't like it.

I don't believe we have as much power in life and death as we'd like to think. What happens to a community when something bad happens to someone they consider "good", is the realization that if it can happen to them, it can happen to me. And that is scary. You cannot be careful enough, fearful enough to thwart death. God has the ultimate decision in life and death. He absolutely had the power to save my daughter and your loved one. He did not. Can you be careful enough, smart enough, or rich enough to avoid cancer? No. That causes me to believe that God has his hand in all of creation and that to God, there are no accidents. Everything on earth is done with all-knowing God's permission. John 10 says that Satan has come to steal and to kill and to destroy, but God has come to give life everlasting.

So, why do bad things happen? I don't know exactly. I do know that God has given us free will to choose and has allowed evil into the world. I also know that bad things and hard times have come on every generation. From the beginning of creation in the bible, Adam was not the first to die, although he was the oldest. Cain was not the first to die, although he was a murderer. So from the very beginning, what makes sense to our minds, what is "fair" does not happen. Who was the first to die? It was Abel, the "good" one. So… God, bad things happened to good people even in

Genesis? I'm sure if this were a real conversation with God, he wouldn't direct me to Adam and Abel, but rather to the cross. Jesus who was perfect was murdered on the cross in his thirties. There is no better example of injustice! He is the example of "bad things happening to good people" and God the Father had to endure the pain of sacrificing his only son. So does God know how I feel, how you feel? Of course He does. Jesus prayed to his Father in heaven, "Lord if there be any other way, take this cup from me." God did not; there was no other way. As I am reminded of this, I take an extra helping of humble pie and fall to me knees. God tells me, "Heather, there really was no other way."

I choose to believe that if God allowed it, then I will accept it. He knew the day Emma would be born, and he knew the day she would die. Psalm 139 says "There is injustice all over the world." God does not promise us a long life without pain. In fact he says in John 16:33, "In this world you will have trouble. But take heart! I have overcome the world."

Bad things will continue to happen to good people; to all people. Let us be the hands and feet reaching out to those as they encounter tough times. Life is hard, but God is good.

Why would God allow this if He loves you?

I find this question especially tough for those of us who had great parents. Because if our earthly parents loved us, protected us, shielded us from harm, then if God is supposed to love us more than them, why isn't He protecting us? God's word reminds me in Isaiah 55:8 that "My thoughts are not your thoughts, neither are your ways my ways".

This question also reminds me of when kids wonder why we scold them or punish them if we love them. And we all know the answer, right? "It's for your own good!" How can punishing me be good?

My spin on this is that tragedy is not punishment; it is God using what will make me the best person possible to fulfill my ultimate purpose. I wish God would have asked me how I felt about this, but He didn't. Sometimes I feel like I was "better" before. I wasn't rebellious. I was serving. I was sharing my faith. I was happier, and might I add, perkier!?

And God says to me, "Heather, this is not just about you and your faith." (Actually it's not about you at all!) This is about the hundreds of people that might be touched or inspired by your courage. God also reminds me of the strength He has given me; He has equipped me to do this. I don't want to, but I can and I will. And one more thing, it is only once I am stripped of everything, do people not see me, but Christ.

Just as our children are only capable of seeing what is right in front of them, so that is true with us and God. We do not have the capacity to fully understand why. We can only see ourselves today at this moment in history. And to be honest, if I knew why, if God explained everything to me, it really wouldn't change my broken heart. The void of Emma would not be less. I would still ache for my little girl.

So, with a gigantic leap of faith, I believe that God still loves me. I believe that He is still in control and hasn't made a mistake. And a step further…I turn the faith I have into trust. I trust that God knows better than me.

Do you just have "blind faith" no matter what?

1. I do not have blind faith no matter what.
2. I am not happy and content in all circumstances.

I would say that an example of someone with blind faith would be someone who perhaps goes to church every week because they think they are supposed to, recites the same passages and prayers, does their "duty" in faith and goes on their merry way. They do not spend time with God. They do not know Him. And the bible says in Matthew 7:21-23 that when they die, God will say, "Flee from me for I never knew you". They may say to God, "Lord, Lord but I believed in you". The bible says that even the devil and the demons believe that God exists. It is not enough to *believe* there is a God.

Contrary to "blind faith" there is "active faith." An active faith requires a lot of verbs- seeking, asking, pursuing, wondering, questioning, rejoicing, weeping, longing, listening, praying, studying, trusting, finding. An active faith forms a relationship with God. One that asks Him why He would do this to my family and me; a faith that gets frustrated; a faith that asks questions; a faith that listens. I have even been known to be sarcastic with God. I've asked Him, "Do you call this blessedness?" "Why should I pray if you're going to do what you want anyway?"

I believe that only during active faith, talking to God, can He give me the answers I desire. Like, "Sshh Heather…Be still and know that I am God." Psalm 46:10

Just as with any relationship, there are ups and downs. There are times of deep love and times of deep disappointment. My hope is that my relationship with God is demonstrated through this trial. God is not some deity in the sky that I don't know. I do know Him, and I trust Him. He wants to know and have a relationship with everyone, with you.

John 10:27 says, "My sheep hear my voice, and I know them, and they follow me."

Through prayer and study God offers peace and clarity. The bible promises that if we seek truth in Christ we will find it. This has been true in my life.

I still wish God wouldn't have entrusted me with this burden. The fact is that this is my cross to carry. Blind faith, no. Active faith, yes. I will carry this cross. I may even grumble and complain along the way, but I will follow Christ forever.

God hurt my feelings!

If I am honest with my feelings, there is a part of me that is disappointed in God so to speak. He hurt my feelings when He allowed my Grandma to be killed by a drunk driver. He hurt my feelings when He did not choose to heal my dad, from cancer. More let downs came with the deaths of my aunt and uncles (all of those people in their 40's-50's) and then my daughter…really God? Where are you?

During this same time of grief, I had observed many other losses: a good family friend named Jim Cantrell who was a mentor to Matt and I, my sister's friend Laney Mota who was killed in a car accident, a little girl named Bailey Rocha in my Sunday school class who lost her battle with cancer, Brenda Durkin and Rick Lunsford, friends from church who lost their battles with cancer, and Zach Nelson, a young man who God did not choose to save.

I am fixing my feet firmly in the ground, crossing my arms, and shouting "God, I don't understand why you wouldn't want to spare our heartaches. These were all God-fearing families who trusted you, who still trust you."

The notion of longsuffering is frustrating for me. As I study people in the bible who God loved and used, He didn't spare them from longsuffering. Abraham and his wife waited on God for several decades to have a baby and then God asked Abraham to sacrifice his child on the altar! (God did spare the child and Abraham from that request) But, Why God? Why one extra day of heartache? God led Moses through a long road of suffering and persecution. And Job, the only righteous one in the land, God allowed Satan to test him and strip him of everything he had. In some ways, these stories help me, and in other ways they frustrate me. They cause me to study the heart of God. Some days this doesn't seem loving at all; in fact it seems mean! And then I am reminded that God used suffering to position these men for great things. Their stories would have been different without suffering, and they may have never been molded into God's finest without it.

James 1:12 states, "Blessed is the man who perseveres under trial, because when he has stood the test, he will receive the crown of life that God has promised to those who love him."

Romans 5:4 says, "Not only so, but we also rejoice in our sufferings, because we know that suffering produces perseverance, perseverance, character; and character, hope.

And finally the verse that I say with sarcasm oozing from my lips, "Consider it pure joy, my brothers, whenever you face trials of many kinds, because you know that the testing of your faith develops perseverance. Perseverance must finish its work so that you may be mature and complete, not lacking anything." James 1:2-3

So, perhaps suffering isn't mean at all, but rather love? God's word talks of how we are catapulted up to a new level of trust, faith, of service, and of love once we have suffered. He positions us to do His will through our trials. I say to God often, that I am done growing (not to be confused with having arrived)…I don't want more character…Please let me be!

I guess the hardest thing for me spiritually is that my idea of my "Savior" has been dispelled. I imagined a Savior coming to the rescue to save me and protect me from harm and heartache. When He doesn't, I feel like He is not trying to spare me from heartache and that truth bothers me. Our loved ones who have died have actually been saved from the cruelty and pain of this life. Isaiah 57:1 says, "The righteous perish, and no one ponders it in his heart; devout men are taken away, and no one understands that the righteous are taken away to be spared from evil." They are in heaven. I also would be remiss to say that God hasn't come to "save" me. Of course He has. He has given me strength; He has wrapped me with a blanket of peace. I would be a different person if my "Savior" wasn't with me. So, as I mature a little, I slowly have to give away the fantasy of a "Savior" that I've created in my own mind who comes to save the day.

Do I allow my heartache to break my spirit? Or do I say to God, "God, I trust you. I do not understand why you would allow so much sadness in my life and in the lives of others. I really wish you wouldn't have. I believe you are a sovereign God who is in control even if it doesn't feel like it."

In our times of suffering and disappointment, even with God, it is okay to have real feelings. God knows them anyhow. It's okay to feel like God didn't do what we had hoped he would have. The important thing is not to allow the feelings to overshadow the truth and the life of who Jesus Christ is and always will be.

This poem was given to me just days after losing Emma. It was written by Katie's friend Laney, who was in Katie's bridal party along with Emma. She was killed in a car accident one year later on July 4, 2011. The words- as touching as they are- have carried a more profound meaning to me after Laney's passing.

I'm so tired but can't seem to sleep
This song below is the only reason not to weep
I don't understand why God took you
Emma Grace it really seems untrue

A beautiful soul so young and naïve
Would have grown happy to believe
In the God her parents truly trust
Though this appears to be so unjust

That he would leave her two brothers
A mother, a father, and many others
With nothing but memories filled with smiles
I know we will forever cherish it through the trials

Please Emma help us to all be strong
And know you're in a place where there is no wrong
All dolled up with huge bows in your hair
And helping our God do anything to prepare

A place for us up in heaven with you
So we can come and live there too
In a place where we can live in peace
With our Lord where all our trials will cease

To everyone who feels the pain
And genuinely know you'll never be the same
Just keep in mind we'll all meet again
In the air we'll see our friend

In happiness we'll all feel the love
And we'll see her smile together above
Together we'll know the reason why
Our Father in heaven took her to the sky

<3 Laney
July 11, 2010

Emma and Laney on both ends

Emma kissin' "T"

Our last family photo with Emma

What Staying Mad at God Really Means

One thing that I have learned from all of the pastors at Harvest Community Church is that God is big enough to handle our anger. He can hold our frustrations, disappointments, and animosity. It is completely valid to be "mad" at God. It is just important that we don't *stay* mad at God.

As I have talked with several women regarding this issue, it has been made clear to me what staying mad at God really means. It really means, "You are the cause of my heartache and so for that I don't want to have anything to do with you." From experience I can say that the anger comes from such a deep disappointment that God didn't intercede or answer our prayers.

One afternoon when I was talking with my mom, who is deeply rooted in her faith, she said that she didn't really care about going to church anymore. She said, "I will always believe, but right now I'm just mad."

I listened to her; I even shared some of the same feelings. And then I said, "Mom, I think you are mad at the wrong person. God did not cause all of this pain in our lives and in the lives of others. God is a loving God who never intended for sin and death in the first place. God is the one who is sustaining you right now."

Don't get me wrong, I've been in the ring with God more than a few times. One time in church the band was singing a song with the lyrics, "Because of you I can dance, because of you I lift my hands, Because of you I can sing, I am free". I remember feeling like I was boiling over with anger. I remember thinking, *No…actually…God…Because of you I can't dance, and because of you I can't sing, and because of you, I'm not free. That's right God, you could have changed this for me and you didn't, so I can't sing. Thanks for nothing.* (Yikes!)

John 10:10 says, "The thief does not come except to steal, and to kill, and to destroy. I have come that they may have life, and that they may have it more abundantly."

This verse reminds me that Satan was the one who came to kill, and God comes soon after to pick up the pieces and to offer restoration and life. I know that Satan wanted to use Emma's death to destroy me and my faith. Instead, God has lifted me to a place where He will turn this tragic event into something beautiful.

I'm not talking about the core of our beliefs or our salvation. I am talking about "leaning". Few people would say that they choose Satan. However, if you do not choose God, by default you are choosing Satan. There is no gray area, ho-hum, neutral being out there. There is good and there is evil, the light and the dark.

I'm still sad and maybe you are too. I still wish God would've answered my prayer to begin with. I wish he would've interceded and saved my daughter. He did not. That places the ball in my court. By staying mad at God, Satan celebrates, and I just can't knowingly be a part of that victory.

Do you believe good will ultimately come out of this tragedy?

Romans 8:28 says, "All things work together for good to those who love God."

I do believe that God will fulfill His purpose and ultimately good will come out of this tragedy and others. I have already seen good come out of it. I believe that Emma may not have impacted nearly as many people if she had lived to be 80 years as she did in her 2 short years.

Her legacy is causing me to act on God's purpose for my life in writing this book, in ministering to others, and ultimately refocusing my life on the ultimate prize of eternity rather than the emptiness and materialism of this world.

Losing Emma will change me forever. It will change Matt and the boys forever. We will become different people because of it. Our choice lies in if we want the *different* to be *better* or *worse*.

The greater good thankfully, stretches beyond our immediate family. The lives in people we know and don't know have been impacted for good as a result of her death.

Nothing will ever feel as "good" to me as having Emma here with me. God will trade beauty for ashes. I want the name Emma Grace Vargas to put a smile on faces. I want the successes of our family to represent the possibilities in Christ; the perseverance in fighting the good fight. I want her legacy to remind everyone to shine their lights even in darkness.

The only way for me to put one foot in front of the other each day, is for me to believe that good will come out of this. Too much pain as been carried for it not to transfer into good somehow; Whether it is the awesome good in someone changing their life for Christ, or a simple good in someone appreciating their children more, hugging them and giving them grace when they don't deserve it, then it feel likes the pain is a little more purposeful.

I would urge anyone who is looking for the "good" to come out of something bad to take an active role in making it happen. I believe that we can be active roles in making the good happen. Our hearts and minds must actively seek the good, and expect nothing less. It is then, that I believe God has fertile ground to work his miracles in our lives and in the lives of others.

Not My Will, But Thine

"Pray for God's will. Nothing More. Nothing Less. Nothing Else." Dr.Ray Pritchard

A significant part of my disappointment with God was that He didn't follow my "plan". I had a good plan; an honorable one.

I was raising my family; we were teaching our children about God; Matt and I were serving in the church; we were looking to begin a small group on marriage. Why wouldn't God love our little life and leave us the hell alone? (Wow did I really write that in my faith chapter)

About seven months before Emma died, Matt had a vasectomy. Our family was complete and we were blessed. This caused even more confusion for us, because we thought, "God why didn't you prevent the surgery if you knew what was coming? And even more if you knew our hearts?"

After losing Emma, Matt and I prayed for another baby. It was our heart's desire. We realized that another baby would not replace Emma, but we had room to still love and nurture another child. I find this conversation intriguing because no one thinks anything of it if you lose a spouse and remarry, but if you lose a child and want another one, you are somehow "replacing them?"

Anyhow, back to wills. Matt and I tried to align ourselves with God's will. We didn't want to force the issue or throw money at it. We flirted with the idea of a reversal, of adopting, and of foster care. No options were ruled out for us. We wanted the yoke to be light and we believed that if God had a child in any capacity that we were to care for, that they would end up in our lives.

We also felt like because we were being so obedient, that God would give us our desires even if that meant a miracle. This confused me because I have always been taught that God gives us the desires of our hearts, and that if you have faith the size of a mustard seed, you can move mountains. I prayed about my confusions. "God, I just don't understand why you wouldn't want to give me this." I have made peace with the fact that Emma is with you. Now a little joy for me! Hello?

We were trying to be patient, but we were not getting any younger, and the boys kept mentioning another baby. Jayden wanted us to have a baby, a baby boy that he could teach. Jayden said, "No baby can replace Emma because she is the only one who would call me JayJay." Tyler wanted us to adopt. I asked him if he wanted us to adopt a boy or a girl, he said, "I don't know, we'd have to see their personalities!" Their responses comforted me because I knew they came from a healthy place. They were not looking to "take in" a two-year-old little girl.

We decided not to do anything for at least a year, and then after a year we would see if we were being led in one area or another. At that time, we started to make phone calls about the vasectomy reversal and adoption. We felt like the doors kept closing on us with fost-adopt, adoption, and the reversal. We could "pay" for any of the options, but that didn't feel the same as being confident that it was the right decision.

As I was talking one day with a friend who was missing her granddaughter, I said to her, "Your happiness cannot be contingent on having your granddaughter or not having your granddaughter." The heavens opened for me. People, even children, are blessings, but should not be our sole source of happiness. (Oh, God, I get it, my happiness cannot be contingent on having Emma or not having Emma.) Peace and happiness must come from within. Dr. Pritchard says, "Happy are the people who hold lightly the things they value greatly."

God was teaching me that I was transferring my joy and peace from Emma into another child to restore me. And I learned that, **He will never give me what I want until all I**

want is Him. God did not want another child to be my Savior. He wanted to be my Savior!

In addition, He was positioning me to disciple women. This was not in my plan. I wanted to run the Christmas program at church, and now that was too painful for me. And God said, "No, I am using you and your circumstance to inspire and teach others." I am calling you to something different. I felt like God was telling me that my life was good, but with that comfortable life, I may not have reached out in the way that I will now.

The day these things were revealed to me, I went home from work with a very heavy heart. What about me God? Don't you care what I want? Do you just expect me to pour myself emotionally into others? I went into the backyard alone, and in the pool, in that spot, it was full of feathers. I cried. "Ok God, I don't know what you are doing, but I will follow this path. I will trust that this path will bring me joy."

Some days I find myself having conversations with women about grief that I would have never talked to otherwise. Some of these women have sought me out because of something they read in the newspaper. They have questions. They are struggling with life as well. Although I don't feel like I have it all together and I certainly don't think I have all of the answers, somehow I have been able to help. Sometimes it is related to grief and raising kids, and other times it's related to just hard-luck life. In any capacity, I believe that the more that we can rely on and relate to one another, the better we will all be. I don't want to know these things. I want to just be an immature, thirty-something, flaky, flighty woman! One day I was driving home from work crying, "God if you made me such an expert on parenting that people seek me out for advice, then why would you take my child?" It's as if sometimes I don't value the wisdom I have gained because it is too late for me.

If Jesus himself struggled with the will of God, should we be surprised if we too struggle with it?

A baby or child may or may not be in our future. My peace and my happiness are no longer dependent on it. Matt and I are open to welcoming a child in any capacity. We will also be at peace if that doesn't happen. God has designed me. He knows what will bring me joy. I can only draw from my knowledge and experience up to this point, but God can see beyond today. Why would I want my will and desire to be at odds with the one who created me and gave me the desires? He will take me to places of peace and joy that I don't know yet. I will yield my plan, my will for His.

Initial Prayers and thoughts

God,
You know my heart.
You know what's best.
You decide. I'll do it.

First day of grief class. This is not a group I want to be a part of. The wounded, broken-hearted. I don't want to have this in common with anyone. I want to go back to my yesterdays when life was light and my joys complete. I'm like a wounded puppy, just lifting his eyes every now and then.

So, God, is this really the blessed life? Why have I been obedient? I suppose I thought it was like insurance. Pretty sad when I feel like AAA is more dependable. Okay forgive me for that one. Matt keeps telling me that God is not Santa Claus. I suppose I should listen.

I have never been this unhappy. Will I rise?

I lie in bed with Emma's blankets and bb's. Her scent is on them. I am going to be sad the day her scent gone. I hug them as if I am hugging her.

Rainy day in June. I want to run away.

Sitting in T's nails. I'm remembering one year ago sitting in this very chair with Emma on my lap. I was getting my toes painted yellow for Ty's championship game. Emma squealed, "Mee too?? My toes too!! I asked the lady how much and she said five dollars. She painted Emma's toes and called her toes "Barbie toes". Today Tyler is trying to talk me into purple for his team, but I can't do it. I settle for salmon and go home with knots in my stomach.

God

Perhaps you'll work on our behalf. I want the land of milk and honey. I'm not done nurturing a little one. We have the capacity to love and care for another child. Of course, Emma is what we want. With that not being possible, Lord, please bless our family. Send us a baby with a smile that can light up a room; that the boys will fall in love with. Restore happiness in our home. We will give you praise. I don't want to seek this on my own. I don't want to force this and throw money at this and do it my way. Your way is easy and light. Let it come from you and Matt and I will wait on you. We believe that you will bestow favor upon us. And please kiss Emma for me and tell her that I miss her more than anything! I count the days to be reunited with her.

The end of summer is upon us. The boys were begging me to go swimming with them today. Breathe, breathe; don't react. Don't be crazy. I didn't want to stick a toe in that pool, but their faces of joy want their mom back. I did it. As I dove into the pool, my tears blended with the chlorine water. As I swam deep into the pool, sun beams met me at the bottom of the pool; a ray of light, perhaps a sign from Emma telling me that "It is ok mom, swim with my brothers." The pool will never be a source of joy for me, however I must still be present and not take the joy away from the boys or others.

Dear God,

Thank you for giving me the strength to work and take care of my family. I know that it is not my strength, but yours. Thank you for the sunrises and sunsets that remind us of the glorious place Emma is in. Thank you for friends and family who love us and support us. Thank you for my boys who give me a deeper calling to move forward and truly live. Lord, help me to see the good. Help me to not be jealous of other families who have their children. Remind me of how blessed I am and how your ways are not like mine (but better). Continue to give me the peace that surpasses all understanding; the contentment that settles my spirit. Show me what's next. Give me a glimpse into the future. Tell me what to do. God, I miss Emma so much. I am trusting you. I miss my family as it was. Comfort me Lord.

If any of you are joyous, you should sing praises to the Lord, those of you who are suffering, he should pray.

That's how I feel. I love God. I'm not in a place to stand and dance. I just need to pray and think and meditate.

If we didn't have suffering in this world, we wouldn't want it to end. We would be like Lot's wife who wanted one more look. It is once we have suffered that we realize how much we need and look forward to God's perfect eternity. I don't want anything in this world anymore- just Christ and my family in heaven.

God,
I feel like I need time to grieve. I feel like I have been too busy to grieve. Please make available the time I need. I so want to be home looking at Emma's things, crying for her, praying. I go to work and then home with the activities of a family. The weekend is the same. Help me to set aside 'me time' to grieve the loss of Emma.

And thank you for guiding me to my dad's Saints jacket today! Wow, what a treat!

Thank-you God for working out time for me to grieve on Fridays! I will not busy myself during this time. I will just feel...even if it doesn't feel good.

Lord you have my heart and I will search for yours.

I am mad. I didn't realize it before. Today I am mad that I don't get to care for Emma. I feel mad at God. I feel like he has placed this incredible burden on me. I know he didn't cause Emma's death, but he certainly allowed it. That makes me mad. I always thought that the good Lord would protect us. As I write those words, I feel guilty, because He is protecting us and our life is still so much better than millions around the world.

I feel like I have lost my past and my future and I'm stuck in the present trying to forge ahead day by day.

I want a little girl- more specifically my little girl. That hurts... A lot.

Last year on this day, Emma was the flower girl at Katie's wedding. Today a memory. That is crazy. I want her now. I want to see her grow. I want to take care of her.

I cry in church almost every Sunday...guess what? The church is for hurting people! Why do people feel like they have to have it together to be at church? How can anyone help or pray for one another if everyone acts perfect?

I had surgery on my leg today. As the nurses and doctor wheeled me in, they were talking to one another. They said, this girl is so healthy. She's not on any meds and her numbers are perfect. Tears streamed down my face. Too bad the doctor's numbers can't see my broken heart.

I went to the cemetery today to have my lunch with Emma. Sigh.

Dear God,
Thank you for giving me a level-head, but no thank you; I would rather be a little crazy and have my daughter.

I found myself on Craig's list today. I've never been there before, but I allowed myself to pretend. I pretended that I could make an offer on a butterfly bench for Emma's room; that I could buy her saltwater sandals and bows. It would seem to be torture, and I was breathing heavily. But it is a fantasy land that I want to live in. I just want my reality as it was. Sigh. (March 2011)

Tyler has become very protective of Jayden and our pets. I know he fears another loss, so he is going to extremes. He doesn't even want our dog going outside to go to the bathroom and he doesn't want Jayden playing basketball in front of our house. Like I said before, no matter how well Matt and I do this grief thing with the boys or not, at the end of the day, there is an incredible amount of trauma involved that we can't change. Yuck!!!

Today the thing I miss most about Emma is brushing her hair and kissing her toes. I would lotion them up after a bath and just massage them. I want to take care of her. I want her here.

Yesterday Jayden and I went to the eye doctor, and there were two little girls there. One kept saying, mommy potty, mommy potty! Jayden looked at me with big eyes. We can forget those conversations sometimes, but then to hear them come out of a two–year-old just sounded so familiar. Without words, we both sighed and thought of our little Emmie.

Every day, everything gets directed back to Emma. When one member of the family is gone, there is a void and a stress. It's like losing a part of your body. You could get by with one arm, but it's not as easy or fun.

I desperately want God to answer and direct us. I still feel so empty. I miss Emma and the boys miss her bunches too!

Summer is very hard; depressed every day. I want to go back to work! I don't like my life and I'm not happy. June 2011

I would've thought that because we did and said all the "right things" that on this end of it, things would be easier. It is not. It is harder. I am very empty. I feel like I've made no progress. I know that I have done a good job parenting the boys through this, but as for myself, yuck.

Turning a corner in grief

I've discovered that in order to begin to live again, you must consciously place yourself in a state of denial. I'm not saying that you should pretend that the loss never happened. It did happen and will never go away. To experience the magnitude of your loss daily though, would strip you of all physical and emotional energy. You need to have moments and hours where grief doesn't consume you...A form of denial, I think?

How is it possible that after a whole house remodel, and almost two years later, I still find one of her baby socks in the laundry every now and then? Some days I find a bottle cap in a bag, or wipies in an old purse...reminders of her very real life and presence.

God,
I know I'll do good things in the future, that good will come, but nothing will replace the loss. I'm not so interested in the good today.
Matt says, "I know that this will be made right one day." I sure hope so.

Tyler made a ceramic mug in boy scouts today...He inscribed, "Family is a gift that doesn't last forever" (ouch)

Breathe, Breathe, Breathe
Hide, Cover, Sleep
I want my old life back.

I never thought there would come a time where looking at pictures would make me feel more happy than sad. There is still a sting, but overall remembering the happy moments and days bring me joy. From the moment Emma was born until she went to heaven, I can honestly say she was just a simple pleasure to be around (except when I had to put her in her car seat☺) Even those moments make me smile; the joy of raising a child, the good and the bad, are moments, gifts, from God to be treasured. I'm glad I did.   August 29, 2011

It is well with my soul.

Just returned from the ladies retreat. I was inspired. I thank God for giving me the strength to be there. I am proud of myself. I know I shouldn't be proud, but it felt good to be real with myself and others.

"Even in my weakest moment, I become stronger."

God,
I am weak. I am very weak. I am a sinner and I can do nothing on my own. Thank you for giving me strength and courage. I pray that the strength others see in me will be a reflection of you. Did I really have the life I now live through photographs? Life is hard, God. Help me.

Feeling super encouraged today. I'm feeling honored to be able to reflect God's goodness through this loss.

The sun is shining. It is a new day. Get up and get on with it!

I feel like I can do anything. If I buried my daughter, I can do anything. Yep. Yep. Yep.

I am smiling more. I am laughing with friends and family. God is good. He has turned the ordinary into extraordinary!

"Let yourself feel good again. Laugh with your friends, have fun. Living your life to the full is not betrayal of a memory but fulfillment of a promise to someone who would only want the best for you." Karen Katafiasz

Part 3- Choices

"You are the person who has to decide. Whether you'll do it or toss it aside; you are the person who makes up your mind. Whether you'll lead or will linger behind. Whether you'll try for the goal that's afar, or just be contented to stay where you are."

Edgar A. Guest

Quite Simply, Will you choose despair or will you choose peace?

My simple approach to some of life's difficulties is to make a mental t-chart and list all of the benefits to taking one path versus another. It becomes very clear and a simple, obvious choice to me.

Giving up and staying in bed	Continue to live life as best as I can
Lose my job	Try to go to work
Lose my house	Try to put my children first
Kids lose stability	Try to make my home peaceful
They become crazy	Relationships strengthen
Lose relationships	Other lives are impacted for good
Depression sets in	Move through depression and stages of grief
Rocking in a corner somewhere	**Coming out stronger than before**

The options on the left just never seemed appealing to me. Locking myself in my room wouldn't bring Emma back. Losing my home and becoming crazy wouldn't either. So what outcome does one expect when they choose despair? I think we must think about our choices and what the choices will bring us.

I couldn't find a "gain" for myself or anyone to staying in bed. Now the truth???

Did I feel like staying in bed forever? Yes.
Did I feel like going to work? No.
Did I want to go to carnivals and parades? No.

Did I want to see lots of people at sporting events? No.
Do I have the right to be a shut-in? Yes.

Do the choices on the right seem difficult when you are
broken? Of course they do; but not too difficult for God. I
kept reminding myself of Philippians 4:13, "I can do all
things through Christ who gives me strength." The mama
bear in me kicked in because I knew that my boys have
already suffered incredibly. Everything I limited them to due
to my grief would've been secondary losses for them. They
can cry because they miss their sister, but I didn't want them
to cry because they can't live their lives.

So as you move through difficult circumstances, take an
objective look at what decisions you are making. Write them
down. And write what your payoff is for choosing whatever
you're choosing. Will you be better off by your choice, or
worse off? Only you know the answers to that.

How do you go to work and carry on?

On July 6, 2010, Emma's last day here with us on earth, I had taken her and my niece Shelby to my classroom. I was writing the names of my upcoming students on their desks. Emma ran around my classroom and found a candy jar. She asked for a sucker, and then another, and then another. I finally said, "That's enough", and she said, "One mo pease!" Shelby laughed at her and kept her busy playing and running around the campus. She would visit my friend Anna on that day, and our custodian Debbie too.

The ironic thing is that I am not one of those teachers who works all summer long. I actually try to just enjoy the summer with my family because August always rolls around with lightening speed. The fact that I had chosen to go to my classroom on that now daunting July day, I think pulled me to go back to work. I felt a connection with my new classroom, and the new students who were a hard to teach, hard to reach bunch once I prepared their supplies. I was also aware of the hard lives many of my students have…harder than mine. If they can come to school every day with the adversities they have, then I can pull it together too. I can't model giving up to my students or my own children.

As my personal and professional life collided after July, I had a decision to make. Obviously, I didn't "feel" like going to work. I did think of my students and how a stream of subs wouldn't be good for them. I also had to evaluate my future. I had come to the decision that quite frankly, I was too young to "throw in the towel". I still had a family to support.

I was also afraid to be a stay at home mom for the first time in my life when I didn't have any little ones at home. I knew that it would push me into a depression. It probably would have caused guilt to come with that as well. So what do you do when you can't work and you can't stay home?

I had come to the decision that going back to work in August would be hard, but going back to work in December or February would be hard as well. The more space you put between yourself and others, the more distance that is created, and the harder it becomes to face the music. I just kept reminding myself that I was surrounded by people who loved me and that they were not there to judge me. I knew by their actions and words that their hearts were breaking for me.

So, the first teacher day back was hard. I did it. I was unusually quiet. Everyone was great in how they treated me. Compassion in their eyes was evident. I remember walking into my classroom and I noticed three sucker sticks. I sobbed. The life of Emma was still in my room. She had colored on my whiteboard and scattered books. It felt like it was yesterday. My life would never be the same again.

The first day of school proved to be one of the hardest of my life. I dropped the boys off at their school and sobbed all the way to the car. I passed the kindergarten line and the realization that I will not have a kindergartener ever again really hit. I cried on the drive from Crowslanding to Gustine. I had to pull into a gas station because I was sobbing uncontrollably. I made it to work. I stayed in the parking lot crying for another hour. (Fortunately since my class is intervention, I didn't have students on the first day) Friends told me that I should just go home. I knew that walking on campus, being in my classroom, and dealing with the emotions of it all would be better on that day without students than when I was faced with students the following day. So I stayed.

Days passed. I felt my grief boiling over by the end of the week. I started to feel a need for time to grieve honestly. I looked into disability, but it was an all or nothing proposition. I just wanted one day a week to be a grieving mom, to go through her things, and to be crazy. I talked with my principal Donna about this. She was supportive and recommended that I write a letter to the board. So I did. By the end of September, I had requested Fridays off to grieve. I would use my sick days and plan and schedule the same sub every week. This time proved to be life-saving. I honestly don't think I could have done it without time to properly grieve and just be without worrying about the impact I was having on the boys.

Work was not always easy. Some days I would be fine, and others I was a mess. I remember one day when I walked into the staff lounge only to find a bright pink flower bowl. It was from Emma's birthday. I brought it to work the year before with snacks and forgot to take it home. Just seeing the physical reminder of Emma and her birthday at work caused me to break.

Students would ask me how many children I have; a student in my class was named Emma; Emma was the main character in our reading selections; and I even struggled with whether or not to have pictures of her in my room. I just desperately wanted my life to be as it was.

I would not say that going back to work is the best thing for everyone who is dealing with loss or difficulties. But it was just the best thing for me to do, to have a reliable constant in my life. Emma permeated every aspect of my life other than work. It was the place I could go and do "my other life".

If you are grieving or struggling, I recommend being proactive in choosing what is best for you. Staying home, working, working part-time, and disability are all options that are there. No one is going to approach you and give you a plan for your life. You need to do that. Be in charge of your life, and when you do what is best for you, it is the right thing to do.

Where does your strength come from?

"I can do all things through Christ who gives me strength" Philippians 4:13

"He gives power to those who are tired and worn out. Even youths will become exhausted and young men will give up. But those who wait on the Lord will find their strength. They will soar high on wings like eagles! They run and not grow weary. They will walk and not faint." Isaiah 40: 29-31

You may be thinking that this should be in my "faith" section, but faith is a choice. I'm not "lucky" to have faith. I have chosen it. It is available for everyone. The wisdom and strength that I have been given during this time is a result of my faith. I am not superwoman. The same human reactions that you might suspect during loss are the same for me minus God's provision.

Once you choose to believe and trust that there is a power greater than yourself, you can find peace in whatever situation you're dealing with. Without it, there is much cause for dissention, disappointment, guilt and bitterness, because all that happens, the good and the bad, rests in your lap; Having the world as your oyster doesn't sound too bad until your life doesn't turn out as you had planned.

I am confident that my life would be very different today, if I didn't believe in God. If I didn't believe that He has my daughter. If I didn't believe that redemption is coming. If I didn't believe that there is purpose to tragedy. If I didn't believe that the bible and its promises are true. If I thought that there really wasn't anything after we died, I would be no different than the hundreds of other grieving mothers in the psych ward banging my head against a wall.

As is the common thread of this book, my strength, my wisdom, my ability to shine in darkness is because of God. I am not a strong person, but with Christ all things are possible.

The lyrics to a Matthew West song, "Strong Enough" have really ministered to me during my healing.

You must, you must think I'm strong, to give me what I'm going through.
Well forgive me, forgive me if I'm wrong, but this looks like more than I can do...On my own.

I know I'm not strong enough to be everything that I'm supposed to be,
I give up
I'm not strong enough.
Hands of mercy won't you cover me,
Lord right now I'm asking you to be strong enough, strong enough for both of us.

Well, maybe
Maybe that's the point, to reach the point of giving up,
Cause when I'm finally, finally at rock bottom
Well, that's when I start looking up and reaching out.

Cause I'm broken down to nothing,
But I'm still holding on to the one thing,
You are God and you are strong when I am weak.

I'm not trying to sell anybody anything, but when people ask questions about how I do it? My faith and my strength are intertwined. I honestly wish everyone with a broken heart or a broken spirit could find the peace that I have. It's the peace that surpasses all understanding...It's the Prince of Peace.

Choices today will affect our tomorrows

There were several times during the grieving process when I felt like I was depositing something into my future. I always had a sense that the good I choose to do with myself or with the kids would produce a good harvest. I've been keenly aware that my behavior, my actions in front of the kids would change who they would become. No matter how well I do this "grief thing", the reality is that the boys have suffered trauma. I do not have control of that. What I do have control of, is where I can take them from that place.

After the first year, I was very depressed. I had hoped that all of those "good deposits" would've put me in a better place. I still felt empty. I might have even said, "Would I really be worse off now if I went crazy and took drugs to numb the pain?" Of course I would've been worse off, but I felt like because I had done what was right, that God would've just made everything better. I wanted a "miracle-grow" harvest. A year felt like a long time to suffer to me! When you love someone or something, it takes a long time to grieve the loss and to be restored.

I know that the fact that Tyler and Jayden are thriving is an example of "good deposits". I know that the fact that Matt and I have been proactive in our grief is an example of a "good deposit". I'm not sure when we will completely be on the other side of tomorrow reaping the fruit of a good season.

We are all depositing something into our futures. Will what we deposit yield something good or bad? Some days, when I am physically and emotionally exhausted, and I am not really "present" with the boys, I think of how that may affect them. I do not get down on myself, but I am aware of the emptiness I am depositing, and I try to do better the next day. Also, decisions that I make regarding my health will yield a result in the future, good or bad. So, going into the next day, I think about it. How do I want to feel physically next year? And then, what steps do I need to take to feel that way?

I try to remember this principle when I move through the stages of life. I am leaving marks on my children as young adults. What do I want their marks to represent? I am leaving marks on Emma's legacy, on my legacy. I am preparing for a bountiful harvest, a harvest that I will receive when it is time.

Making decisions based on mind instead of emotions

This has been an area where God has equipped me to be able to make decisions based on my mind instead of emotions. It is not that I do not "feel" like everyone else, but I don't let my feelings steer my ship.

My mind is what pushes me in the direction to do things that my heart does not want to do. My heart does not want to participate in anything fun, but my mind reminds me that it is necessary for the boys and myself. My heart doesn't think I can ever be happy without Emma, but my mind tells me happiness comes in different forms and I need to look for it.

In the emergency room, my heart felt as if it was being torn out of my chest, but my mind looked past Emma and into the eyes of the boys. My mind wouldn't let me be crazy because then I would've been kicked out and restrained. I think it is more common for people to react first and then try to clean up the mess later.

Here are some examples of mind vs. emotions:

- My heart would've caused me to quit my job, but my mind wanted to remain in my home.
- My heart wanted to move, but my mind knew that the boys loved their neighborhood.
- My heart would've filled the pool with dirt, but my mind knew that it wouldn't aid in my healing.
- My heart doesn't want to celebrate holidays; my mind knows that I would be sadder without them.
- My heart doesn't always want to be happy for others; my mind knows it's the right thing to do.

The disclosure here is that it is absolutely exhausting to think this much! It is much easier to let your feelings dictate you're every move. The problem is that your heart lies to you, and you will do things that you will regret because you "were caught up in the moment". I've learned to allow my heart to make little decisions. It's the big ones that have lasting implications.

Learning to exercise this takes practice and wisdom. Have courage, pray for strength, and if you are conscious in your decision making, you will be happier with your results.

A Grieving Wife

85% of couples who lose a child divorce. I think generally that both husband and wife are so broken after losing a child that they don't have much to give to one another. After experiencing this loss, I can understand how that can happen.

Just as is true with all marital issues, communication offers an authenticity that proves to be successful. The first two weeks after Emma died, we were completely devastated and we had lots of visitors. We were also very involved in the boys' every move. I began to think about Matt and his needs as a man. I thought about how my needs- especially in regards to intimacy- felt very different from his right now. I sat him down and said, "Listen, I know you are grieving too, but I also know that you have needs. I continued, "I am completely consumed with the loss of Emma and right now sex is the last thing on my mind…But, I promise that I will continue to meet your needs…Just don't expect me to be cute!" A load was taken off of him. He was like, "Thank God!" Surprisingly, he was so grateful that I even recognized that he might have needs, that he became even more compassionate and sensitive toward me.

As a wife, it really doesn't matter if we think our husbands "deserve" it or if they should "want" it. The fact is they do. Their continued sex drive does not lessen their grief. They are not less sad than you because they think about sex. They really can't help it. (You're welcome husbands☺)

Despite grief, we all need to continue to nurture the other relationships in our lives, especially our marriage. It will not just sustain itself on its own. I thought about our future and how I needed to think beyond my immediate emotions. Also, physical intimacy proved to be good for both of us.

In addition to sexual intimacy, communication in other areas kept us on the same page as well. We talked constantly. We talked about our grief. We talked about Emma and the boys. We talked about faith. We went to grief class together. We felt like we were a united force to overcome this challenge together. We did…at least for the first year.

After the first year, we had discussed everything. There was nothing else to be said about the loss of Emma. We had spoken of faith and we agreed on all of the "right answers". Now what? I came up empty and sad. The reality that my future had changed was tough. I wasn't happy. I struggled with happiness and I started to not care about anything, including my marriage. I felt like when my family was intact, I overlooked things that bugged me, but now that my family was not intact, the things that bugged me magnified.

I thought about leaving. But then I thought about how our divorce would always be connected to the loss of Emma. I do not want any negative to be associated with her life or death. I wrestled with this for months. I knew that Matt and I were the only two people who shared this loss at this level. I also recognized our marriage as the foundation for the boys' stability. I knew I had to try and put in some work. So I did.

Two broken hearts that grieve differently and heal differently can present a challenge to a marriage. This is one of those times where I think you need to put some of the emotions aside and really think about the decisions you are making. Yes, I am a grieving mother, but I am also a wife. I still won't say that we will live "happily ever after". It is a journey and it is a lot of work.

Once my depression had lifted, our relationship has become easier again. Through my depression I learned that when you feel like you don't have anything left to give because of hurt, you need to at least communicate that. All feelings are valid. Just don't make people guess…especially not men!

I recall one night that Matt and I decided to go out dancing with some friends. As we were driving, I kept thinking, "I really shouldn't be all dolled up; I should not be happy enough to dance". The other voice in my head said, "You have to put yourself out there and try to have fun;

Nurture your marriage. It does honor Emma". When we got there, we saw some people we knew. I felt guilty. I wondered what they were thinking. We decided to just enjoy ourselves and dance. We did; we danced and had a great time…until a slow song came on. The song, "Butterfly Kisses" started playing. Matt and I went out to the dance floor. Our legs hardly moved. Tears flowed down our cheeks. We stayed out there crying during the whole song and then we concluded that it was time to go. Sobbing, I told him I wanted a big, fat dessert. We went to BJ's restaurant. Laney, Katie's friend was working. She rushed over to us and gave us a hug. She brought me out a giant "Pazookie" dessert and she gave Matt a free steak dinner! Comfort food indeed. We learned that night that although it felt good to have fun together, we were still broken.

I suppose in a marriage there are always roles to be played, and there are times when one partner seems to hold the two together. Sometimes this has been me, and sometimes this has been Matt. During our grief, Matt was absolutely the rock and the strength that led. He led our family spiritually. He said almost daily, that "This would be made right". He was in prayer asking for guidance and lifted spirits for all of us. He nurtured us. His heart broke for himself, but I think more for me. The ebb and flow of marriage causes ups and downs. While our family was in turmoil, he displayed strength and character. The fruits of my words in this book also represent his faithfulness to God and to our marriage. I'm very thankful for that.

Be Realistic about what you Are Grieving For

This lesson has required much control of my mind. I hope I don't come across as insensitive, but I would rather be helpful and save you from unnecessary grief than to not offer this perspective at all.

Here we go. It is important to know what we are grieving for specifically. It is important to put the emotions into a compartment where they are identified. This will save us from fanatical grief.

For example, related to Emma, there are several things that I mourn for.

- A child
- A daughter
- The baby
- Our relationship
- Her relationship with others
- The hopes I had for her future

Different things trigger grief in different areas. Losing a child can cause universal emotions in that we all love our children and we want all of them. Emma being my only daughter will bring upon grief related to mother/daughter activities. The fact that she was the last child, the baby, causes me to miss nurturing a little one and leaves my arms empty. Some days I grieve for that. I mourn for the specific relationship I had with her, who she was in my life. Some days my heart breaks for who she was to others, Matt and the boys, and extended family and friends. I want to be able to bring her with me to events where we as a family had such a good time. And finally, there is a part of me that grieves for the loss of her future, and mine. My heart aches when I think about her not going to kindergarten, not signing her up for

111

dance or t-ball and so many other things I wanted to share with her. This is where it gets tricky.

I've learned how to grieve for what is, not what is not. I will cry because that little two–year-old lit up my life and I miss her, but is it really fair or profitable to cry because she is not a cheerleader? What if she hated cheerleading? I don't know about you, but I have enough "real" grief, I don't need to create more in my mind.

It is common for people to mourn their child's wedding day. I think weddings are generally special days to celebrate, so we are sad that we won't share that moment with them. I understand those feelings, but for me, I don't know who that person is. I don't know the young woman Emma would've become so it takes a lot of work to grieve for something that is not. Not to be antagonistic, but what if she never chose to get married? What if she didn't or couldn't have children. We really shouldn't mourn a future we have no idea about.

My heart tugs at my insides when I want to buy her something; when I wish she was still here growing in our family. There will always be the "could've, should've." There will always be, "Emma would be __age now." I wonder about who she would've become. I wonder some days if she would've liked sports more or dance and cheerleading more? It is completely normal to ponder the hopes and dreams we had for our children, as long as *our* dream for them doesn't consume us.

The "real" things that we miss are many. Focusing on those demonstrates how much we miss that person in our lives. Creating fantasies just adds more unnecessary grief to our already broken hearts.

Be present with yourself and know yourself. Know that today I am missing my little girl. Today I miss caring for a toddler. Today I am sad that the reality is hitting that she won't be playing t-ball. All emotions are valid, but the best way to honor and miss your loved one is to mourn who they were, not who you thought they would be.

Happiness is a Choice

Although Emma made me happy, she did not make me a happy person. I was a happy person before I had Emma. My joy and happiness comes from within. It wouldn't be fair to me to make my happiness the responsibility of someone else. We should not look towards people including our spouses and children to make us happy.

I am not happy with my situation. I might say that I am not as happy as I was before when my family was complete. However, to choose to be unhappy for the rest of my life is a choice and one that affects many people.

I deserve to be happy and joyful and so do you. My body hurts when I'm angry, sad or depressed. You have to look for the joy. Some days that is harder than others. It is a choice nonetheless.

I am not dishonoring Emma's legacy by being happy. I am not discounting the magnitude of her loss. She is perfect in heaven right now. Remaining sad forever will not bring her back, it will just bring me down.

My boys deserve a mom that has joy. A mom that is happy for them and their accomplishments. A mom that does not carry the burden of conditional happiness; like, "My mom was only happy when she had Emma." That hurts.

My mom just returned from a mission trip to orphanages in Guatemala. She spoke of the joy the people had. They have no material possessions, and they live with the basic necessities. Yet these people have more joy than us Americans who have everything!

We search for happiness with things, with success and from people. No thing, no amount of success and no one can make you happy. Your joy must come from within; a spirit of joy and peace.

Proverbs 3:13-14 says, "Happy is the man who finds wisdom, and the man who gains understanding; for her proceeds are better than the profits of silver, and her gain than fine gold."

Choosing happiness is hard to do when we are suffering. It calls for us to dig deep and to seek happiness and goodness amidst struggle. In the beginning of my suffering, I had no happy days. Then I had one happy day a week, and then two happy days a week and the happy days became more frequent. Today, I have one unhappy day a week, and I'm looking to outgrow that day too soon. I will always have moments of sadness, but sad will not describe my state of being.

My mom with orphans in Guatemala

Corporate Grief, Anti-depressants, and Going Crazy

If you choose, there is much to learn about yourself during the grieving process. We know of learning styles. We know of personality styles. Has one considered grieving styles? I've learned that there are different grieving styles to discover as we move through the stages of grief.

After the first year, I discovered something about myself…I don't like corporate grief. I don't want someone to ask me to gather. I don't want an organization to decide "Today is the day to mourn". I don't like group memorials. I feel like the loss of my daughter is such a personal thing, that I don't want to gather to reflect. I don't enjoy a show. Some gain strength in numbers, and some appreciate the coming together to honor, but me, not so much. I am thankful that there are organizations to offer support, and I will recommend several resources available. As I've learned more about myself and my grieving style, I've learned that I don't want my grief to be orchestrated. Organized grief however, is the very thing that some people want and need to bond with a group of people in a similar situation. One is not better than the other; it is a "grieving style."

Pills, pills, and more pills! I am not a doctor or a psychologist and I probably have no merit to offer words on this topic. I choose to write about my experience and this topic with full disclosure that I am not an expert. After losing Emma, some people would offer Matt and me sleeping pills. People would suggest that we check with our doctor to see if anti-depressants were the way to go. We did take sleeping pills on the first two nights after her passing to ensure sound sleep. After two days, we wanted to see what our bodies needed. Did we need help sleeping? Would we be able to sleep on our own? For us, our bodies were so drained physically and emotionally that we went to sleep each night without struggle…and without pills. Next it was time to contemplate a doctor visit. I didn't want to go to the doctor. I didn't want to see people and I didn't particularly want the sympathy. This caused me to put it off. I figured I'd wait until I was desperate. Matt and I chose to go to work without the help from medication. I'm not suggesting that it was the best thing to do; I'm simply stating the facts. Perhaps with the help of anti-depressants, our highs and lows wouldn't have been so extreme. At my lowest point (the summer of 2011) I decided that when August rolled around, if I was still low, then I would make the appointment to hear my options. We did that. Matt and I made the appointment. I didn't want to be numbed from all of life; just the hard parts. As it turned out, due to a busy office and scheduling problems we were never seen. We chose to carry on as we had the previous year. My drive was that I wanted to "feel", even if it didn't feel good. I wanted to feel the good days as well. I have always been pretty healthy emotionally so I could risk the low. To this day, we have never taken medication during our grieving process. I am not stating that as an accomplishment. It is not. I am stating that to communicate our process. I am fully aware that psychologically and chemically, medication is a life-saver to many people. It is not a form of weakness, but rather strength to look into all of your options.

Going crazy; Yep I went crazy. Others expect you to be the same person you were before, only sad. That is not possible. Grief causes you to do things and say things that you would've never otherwise done or said. I remember telling my friend Anna (who doubled as my counselor) that I didn't want to be crazy. She would look at me matter of fact and say, "Well you are." "No! I'm the stable one! I'm the reliable constant! I don't want to be crazy," I would exclaim. I think that this was just one of many stages of grief. I'd like to think that I am not still crazy. Unfortunately the loss goes deep, and with deep loss, comes deep emotions that often cause us to react. What many people do not realize is that in the depths of grief we are looking through the lenses of grief.

What may seem like nothing to the rest of the world may carry a ton of weight with someone who is grieving. I too, Miss Stable, am crazy. Darn grief.

Learn about yourself during the grieving process. What helps you? What doesn't? Is what you are doing for your own benefit or for someone else's? What is your doctor's advice on your health; your mental state? When can you choose to give yourself grace for acting crazy? As is the theme through much of the section on choices, learn about yourself. Reflect. The better you know yourself, the better fit you will choose for yourself.

Part 4- Healing

"Although the world is full of suffering, it is also full of the overcoming of it." Helen Keller

New Buds Emerge

If each of us was a flower, with the stem representing the core of who we are, and the petals representing each of our traits, I learned that for me, loss permeated every aspect (each petal) of my life.

I had expected to lose my happiness petal. I did not expect for my confidence, my peace, my pride, my energy, my appearance and all things to be affected by my grief. They were. I was stripped of everything. It made the loss go deep; deep into the core of who I was, who I am, and who I wanted to be.

I remember looking at a picture from before and thinking, "Who is that girl?" I don't know her anymore. That would make me angry and sad. I liked who I was. I wanted the old Heather back. This is when I had to get 'real' with myself. Who am I? Who do I want to be? I am changed. What does that have to mean for my future?

I could not regrow the same petals from before. I lost them to the damp soil in the earth. New buds have emerged. I realized that although Emma made me happy, she did not make me a happy person. Pondering that caused me to realize that I needed to choose joy for myself because it would benefit me, honor Emma's life, and be in-line with who I really am. It is harder for me to be sad and depressed all the time, than to be cheerful.

Slowly, one by one, the petals have begun to grow. My confidence, peace, and energy levels are on the rise. I can feel parts of the old mixing with the new to create who I am now. I am still broken. I may always look through the lenses of loss. The loss can create good, new petals as well; compassion, empathy, modesty.

I've chosen to be conscious of the petals that are growing. What will they represent? Who am I? Your loss doesn't have to overshadow your growth. So, take a deep breath, and begin to BLOOM!

Today marks 9 months without our sweet Emma.

When I think about life and blooming, I picture that if I were a flower, it has been as if someone plucked all the petals off and stripped me of my leaves.

I have been exposed. I am a vulnerable stem. Limp and wounded, I have remained covered,

Today I still feel wounded and bare, but a little stronger. I may only be a stem, but I am not a limp stem anymore.

I am facing the sun and waiting for my new leaves to begin.

Although I don't foresee petals this season, they will come.

I am confident that my new petals will be brilliant, shining the colors and the faithfulness of Jesus Christ.

Comforts and Difficulties

As has been stated several times, grief is a unique journey. What comforts me may be different than someone else. I have attempted to list things that comfort the grieving heart, as well as the things that may hurt the person who is suffering. This page is for all who want to be helpful in the event of suffering.

Comforts	Difficulties
Cards- The person can read when ready Texts	Phone calls are hard because it may not be a good time
Coming to visit	Avoidance
Saying, "I'm Sorry"	Saying, "I understand" (you don't)
Making and bringing food	Acting like nothing happened
Offering to pick something up for you	PLEASE don't complain about your kids!!! (I would love to be up all night with a crying, whining toddler. Don't take your kids for granted...at least not in front of me!)
Sharing in your sadness	
Flowers and plants are thoughtful	
Be real with them- They have not become an alien since their loss	

Some of the simplest gestures during the first weeks after losing Emma were the most helpful. Friends would text me and say "Hey I'm at Target, do you need anything?"or

"I'm bringing you dinner tonight." Or "What kind of cereal do the boys like? I'm bringing you some." These may seem simple, but they are the exact things that I needed. I wasn't up for going to the store. I didn't want to run into people yet. Although I didn't care about eating or cooking dinner, the rest of my family still wanted to eat.

I read each card that came in the mail. Each card made me cry, and each card reminded me that I was not alone. The compassion felt was huge and very helpful.

Often times people feel like they don't know what to do or say, so they do nothing. Some people would send a card simply with the sentiments, "There are no words." Well that speaks volumes! It says I'm thinking of you, I care about you, I am sad for you, and there is nothing I can say to make you feel better. And guess what? It made me feel better.

Everyone is different, but don't allow your fear or insecurities to keep you from reaching out to the grieving. It can be a very lonely time.

1. Don't stay away! Just because it is uncomfortable, doesn't mean you have the right to avoid the situation altogether. It really sends the message, "I don't care about what you are going through." Even though I know that is not the message people want to send, that is how it can be received. People that choose to do what is uncomfortable in an effort to demonstrate love and support offer much comfort.

2. When people would recognize and acknowledge that I was still hurting, I actually gained strength. Because someone else would mention it, I didn't feel the need to. I would talk of my grief often, especially around those who just wanted everything normal. It was as if I had to scream, "My life is still different, remember?!" I felt like those who would regularly check-in on my grief really "got it" so I didn't need to mention it a lot.

3. Don't act like the deceased didn't exist. Sometimes for fear of "bringing her name up" people would actually omit it from their lips. That would really hurt my feelings! This is an area that probably varies the most from person to person. I loved it if people were having a discussion about babies and they would choose to include me like, "Emma was little wasn't she? How much did she weigh?" That is the most normal of conversations. Please don't act like she never existed and you can't say her name. I would not say to force her name in conversations, but if relevant and if you would've included her or me before, include us now.

4. Don't constantly look at me with pity and sad eyes. I appreciate compassion; however, sometimes just real language is best. For instance, just a "Hey, I've been thinking of you; I know this must be hard" is better than "Hiiiiii." And coddling me like I'm a four year old. I don't really want to be hugged and babied by everyone. I'm sure this is a personality thing that varies.

5. Don't stare at me! I am not a weirdo. After losing Emma, I noticed people looking at me more, essentially watching my every move. I think this could often cause someone who is grieving to retreat even more. Not every move I make is related to my grief. Don't make us feel like freaks by staring at us.

6. If talking or visiting with someone is too hard for you, send them a note. I remember a woman in my grief class who said that nobody talked to her at church anymore. I said to her, it's probably because they just don't know what to say." She said, "Too bad! I don't have tolerance for that! If it's hard for them to just talk to me, they should imagine how hard it is for me to live it!" This is a perspective of someone who lost her husband.

I cannot tell you how to act around everyone, but I will say that the safest thing to do is to just be real. Talk honestly. Speak from your heart. Say, "I'm sorry; I have no idea what to say to you." That is completely valid and compassionate. It's really not about the words or how profound the thoughts. It's about saying, "I'm thinking of you." I think we can all do that.

What Does a Grieving Person look like?

How someone looks while grieving is very personal. It is the thing however, that people use to measure how we are doing. I am the kind of person that wears my heart on my sleeve. If I look good or "together", the rest of my life probably is too. If I look bad, then it is a reflection of that as well. The pictures of our family before Emma died looked like the All-American family; it didn't just look like that, it was. The pictures after Emma died showed its marks of grief. When I was grieving, particularly the first year, I didn't feel like looking together; essentially because I wasn't. I couldn't bring myself to forcing a family photo with fake smiles.

What I didn't expect was for other people to assess my appearance so much. If I looked bad, then people would look onto me with sadness, like "poor thing". And if I looked good, then people would say things like "Wow can you believe she looks normal?" It was as if I couldn't win. I summed it up by deciding that if I felt good, and I wanted to look good, I would look good. And if I was sad or depressed, and didn't feel up to caring, then I wouldn't. I was going to be true to myself and my feelings and others could talk.

There is guilt associated with "looking okay" when you have lost someone. It's as if you are portraying that you are okay and somehow that betrays your loved one. I don't think walking around with a gray cloud above your head honors them much either, but that is what people want to see.

I certainly had a gray cloud the first year. I was gloomy from the inside out. I couldn't wear bright clothes, sparkles, or high heels. Just getting dressed was difficult enough. I also remember the feeling of wanting long-sleeves and sweaters because they made me warm and comforted me, like a blanket.

I also didn't want to hear someone say, "You look cute". As if something like clothes really mattered. When you are grieving, especially the loss of a child, people are intrigued so they watch you. I felt like I was getting enough "attention" from my grief; I didn't want to do anything that could draw more attention to myself.

As I've progressed in my healing, I no longer feel guilty for "looking okay". Some days I still want to be comforted and somber, but for the most part if I feel good, I want to look good. I still have a husband and children and there are many days to live. I want to live large. I want to smile at people. I want to strut my stuff, the kind of stuff that shines from the inside out… If that makes other people uncomfortable, too bad.

Many people would see us at sporting events, birthday parties, or work. We usually looked okay in these situations. What people didn't realize was that if I was going to "show up" to support my boys or attend my niece's birthday party, I wasn't going to make it about me. It is not the appropriate time. If a party or event brought about emotions within me, I would usually deal with those emotions before or after the events so people never really saw me "falling apart". In addition, if I felt good enough to go to work, I was going to do my job. If I couldn't do my job, then I would stay home. It takes emotional strength to know yourself well enough to know what you can or cannot handle. Again, all of the attempts to do any of these things were an attempt on my part to keep normalcy for the boys.

I think it is also necessary for me to discuss the differences in the personalities of private grievers and open grievers. I am an open griever. I will talk of my grief, cry in front of others, be honest with my feelings, and wear my emotions- the good and the bad- for everyone to gawk at. Matt, on the other hand is a private griever. Even weeks after losing Emma, if we ran into someone and they shook his hand and said, "How are you?" he would say, "Great!" with a smile. This bothered me. I would think, "Really, you're great?" Because I knew he wasn't great. I told him, "You can say fine, you can say okay, you can say hangin' in there, but you can't say great!" But he never looked or acted differently in the public eye after our loss. It is not dishonest for some people to keep their very intimate private lives, well private. He simply would not put himself in very vulnerable situations. He was not less sad than me. He didn't grieve less than me. The same things that triggered my grief-triggered his grief, too. He was (and still is) a broken-hearted man, and I a broken-hearted woman. We just handle our grief differently. I would caution everyone to be careful before assessing how they think someone is doing based on the way they look. Grief is internal and very intimate.

The Meaning of Christmas Revealed

As Christmas approached the first year, I knew I had to be proactive to just survive the season. I decided to get a little tree that we would call "Emma's Tree". I asked friends and family to bring an ornament that reminded them of Emma. This was an attempt for me to include Emma in our Christmas traditions. It was also safe for me because I didn't have to "hope" that someone would acknowledge her during the holiday. Having them choose an ornament and put it on her tree would ensure that she would be thought of. We did this at the beginning of December so by the time Christmas day came; I didn't feel like I needed anyone to do anything special. I'm sure this sounds completely egocentric but in the beginning especially, you just don't want others to forget. It was important for me to include a tradition for Emma with the boys as well. I knew that years would pass and they would get older. I just wanted something that would pull us altogether in the Christmases to come.

A local organization called Compassionate Friends holds a candlelight vigil each year for those who have lost loved ones. Our family attended with others from the community. Each year they have a slideshow with pictures and names. There is usually a band and people speak about loss. It is a touching evening, but hard. In addition, our local newspaper, The Westside Index, allows people to submit pictures of their lost loved ones called, "Let their Light Shine". This allows people to memorialize the loss of a child or loved one who is no longer with you for Christmas. It is such an honor. When we opened the newspaper the first year, Emma was at the tip of the Christmas tree. Matt and I cried. She looked beautiful and we were very proud.

One of the hardest things about Christmas was sending our Christmas cards. Do I send one with the four of us smiling? I can't even grasp this new family of four. How do I sign the card? Can I really leave her name off? Can I include it? Can I include her picture? Not sending a card didn't feel right to me either. So I decided to just be honest. I sat down at my computer and started writing. I didn't know what I was going to write, but it all just came and the sad truth landed on the pages. I included that I could not send a card with fake smiles. We were sad. I also spoke of hope. I wasn't trying to be shocking, I just didn't know how else to be.

As I pondered Christmas and the meaning, I learned something at my grief class that really helped me. I heard one of the experts say, "Christmas is the sufferer's holiday". That was great news! I was thinking of Christmas as the holiday for happy people and that wasn't me. But now, with this new perspective, this was a holiday I could celebrate too! A Savior was born! A Savior is here for those of us that are broken! Yeah! That's me!

I've always loved Christmas. I decided that just because I was grieving didn't mean that I suddenly had to start hating Christmas and Christmas music. I love Christmas music; I love shopping; I love the hustle and bustle and all of that doesn't have to change.

Will Christmas ever be the same without Emma? No! Will I ever be quite as jolly? Probably not. I wish I could buy her gifts. I wish her stocking would be filled and not just hung. For now we have her tree and like I always say, "That is the best we can do for her here." On the second Christmas, I was getting her ornaments out. I pulled out some with pictures, a pair of pink patent leather shoes, nail polish, bows, and tic-tac ornaments. I cried. I think the first Christmas I was so numb that I never really "saw" them. They are amazing. One of my favorites is a snowflake from my brother-in-law Randy, with the inscription, "There is only one you; Beautiful you."

As time has passed I have become more present to myself and the boys. I want to have some rockin' good Christmases with them. And best of all, we are celebrating the birth of Jesus. The same Jesus that is spending Christmas with Emma! That is cause to celebrate!

Giving to Others

I would not have suspected grief to be such a lonely, desolate time. I did not think that my ability to give would change, but it did. Suddenly I was very conscious of what I would do and where I would give of myself and my time.

Things that were easy before were now hard. The giving of smiles was selected carefully. The helping hand suddenly felt like the giving of my soul.

This made me angry. How can giving be hard? "God, didn't you like me more before when I was a giver? Now I'm selfish…how can this be good?"

The truth is that I had to keep every bit of emotional strength for myself just to get by. I truly had nothing to give. No smiles, no help, no definite commitments. I would not commit to anything.

I learned that this was a time to receive. I was on the receiving end of smiles, encouragement and support. I received time from others, gifts, and love. It is important to be able to receive. It is what I needed. Eventually I needed less.

As my healing continued, I slowly began to be able to give again. I remember being in a situation where someone else's needs to be confirmed were greater than my needs of sympathy. I knew at that moment that that person's needs were greater than my own. I was able to give. I recognized it as a turning point in my grief.

My restoration is not complete. I still have to think more than I'd like to about things. I am finding places and reasons to give again. I am giving again at work and with my friends and family.

When you experience a grief like this, you essentially have power. At any moment you can choose to break someone with your words or build them up. When my friends have babies and their children, I can offer love and joy for them or I can make them feel uncomfortable and guilty. I know that every time I choose to give love, that the impact for them and for me is much.

I still can't give much at church. I don't feel like the payoff in service, tithing or obedience has protected me. I know that this is a stage of my grief where I am still struggling with God. God has made my giving look different than before. Perhaps I won't give in the area of children's ministries for now because it is too painful, but now I will disciple women, start a small group, or minister to families who are grieving.

I still have a desire to give. God will make provisions for my pain and direct me in the areas of giving that will allow me to fulfill the purpose He has called me for.

If you are grieving, don't feel bad or guilty if you can't give like you did before. This is a season that may look different and it is temporary. If you know someone who is grieving, give them some space and don't put pressure on them to give in the same way they did.

Gluttony, Rebellion, and Feeling Sorry for Myself

For the desires of the flesh are against the Spirit, and the desires of the Spirit are against the flesh, for these are opposed to each other, to keep you from doing the things you want to do. Galatians 5:17

Throughout my healing time, I had some low periods. I remember thinking, "Who cares how I look?" I lost my daughter. Who cares if I eat what I want and never exercise again?" Can I feel any lower than I do right now? This was the beginning of weight gain, loss of muscle mass and even more depression. Just because you have "the right" to not take care of yourself, doesn't mean you shouldn't. My body began to ache. The physical and emotional stress had taken its toll. It caused me to feel even worse.

At my lowest point, I remember thinking "Is this it?" Am I really supposed to be satisfied with the "leftovers" of my life? I love my boys to pieces, but I am not complete without *all* of my children. I didn't see how they could possibly be enough to fulfill me. During the summer after the first year, I got quite depressed and I allowed myself that time to feel sorry for myself.

Another episode included me saying things like, "I've done the right things my whole life and it's not really working for me!" I'm not sure it really matters. In fact, doing the "right things" has not spared me from heartaches. God never seemed to intercede on my behalf so screw it! I thought, "Maybe I'll start popping some pills, or even better and more fun, maybe I'll do something shocking like have an affair! My salvation in Christ is secure, so God, I don't need any extra jewels on my crown…you can have them!"

My justification was that if I couldn't have the family that I had (which I couldn't) then maybe I'll just create a whole new life! That's right. I'll create a selfish, all about me life! I will do what I want when I want! So there!

The problem is…I make decisions based on my mind not my emotions, remember? I thought about what the destruction of our family would do to the boys. I thought about how well they are doing despite their grief; I knew that any other change or trauma could spiral them into a place that I may not be able to rescue them from. I thought about my negative outlook and how I needed to look for the satisfaction of what I had instead of what I wanted.

When we look to other things, substances, or people to restore us, we will come up empty. My mind knows that. Not only will it not bring me satisfaction, it will actually bring me down because of the guilt or other consequential fallouts. We will always be worse off from our bad choices.

So, do I always feel like doing the right thing? No! I want to be a rebel. I want to not care. I want to do something shocking. We all have temptations where our spirit and flesh will fight one another. This is just another example of choice. I won't say that I always have or always will make the right choices. I will however continue to try to yield to my spirit which is the source of goodness and of peace.

Do you relive that night daily? Do you have regret, guilt or blame?

1. I do not relive that night daily. I choose to think about all of the wonderful memories I had with Emma instead of allowing one night to overshadow her life. That night and the events of that night creep into my mind from time to time, but I either dismiss them or choose to think about it and allow for sadness. When people choose to focus on the tragedy rather than the life, they most definitely will live in despair.

2. I have never had a nightmare. I prayed that night that all of the images I saw from the hospital, to the funeral would not be frightening for me or the boys…and they haven't been. I will not allow scary thoughts into my mind so I go to bed clear…I do dream of Emma from time to time, and although I love it, I wake up heartbroken. No nightmares though.

3. Matt and I have never blamed each other or ourselves. Quite simply, I thought she was with him, and he thought she was with me. Period. No negligence. The boys were not around the situation which I am very thankful for so they can't blame themselves either. It wouldn't have been normal for me to say, "Tonight I'm not cooking dinner, I'm just going to follow Emma around." That's when you have to be confident that there really is nothing we would've done differently. I also believe that guilt, blame and fear come from Satan and I don't think any good comes from those emotions.

4. The strangest thing is that Emma never once tried to get in the pool. When you have a pool at your house, children are familiar with it, and they understand the protocol…at least so it seemed. If Emma wanted to swim she would say, "Me swim? My suip? (bathing suit)". Her

favorite by far was not the pool, but the spa. She would squeal, "Spa…meee toooo????" If we told her no, she would go onto something else. She also knew she needed her safety gear on before getting in. She was very smart. She often played outback with us in her playhouse and in her "cozy coupe" car. I am still completely stumped as to how she got outside unnoticed, and then that she would go into the pool. And then…if she did go into the pool, she was by the steps, a large Acapulco shelf where she could've stood up. She did so daily all summer long. There was no splash. There was no noise…no warning. Just in the blink of an eye, all that I knew to be consistent and true of her behavior had changed. Part of what gives Matt and me peace is the fact that nothing about that was normal…it was as if she were lured and silenced. We really feel like the circumstances that transpired truly were out of our control.

5. Some days Matt and I will engage in discussion of regret. Like, stupid dog! If only we didn't have the stupid dog, Emma would still be here. If only we never got the pool to begin with…Maybe I should have just held her and fried tacos (despite the advice from my chiropractor). In the end, those would've, could've, should'ves don't really matter. Do we really have the power to change destiny? I'm not sure. What I do know is that if Emma was meant to live a long life, she would still be here.

If Emma were still here, I would not feel guilty for making tacos while Matt had the kids, so why would I feel guilty just because it turned tragic? Matt doesn't feel guilty because he was helping Jayden to do something for Tyler and he thought Emma was with me. Guilt might be different if we had thrown caution to the wind and allowed her to play by the pool. That is just not how it was. We follow code; we have an alarm. The alarm doesn't do much good however when you bypass it to let the dog out. On occasion I have engaged in feeling guilty for not protecting her more as her mom. In the end, I know that to prosper I need to hold my thoughts captive. I need to choose to not focus on what I cannot change.

Do I blame Matt for not having Emma? No. Does he blame me for not having Emma? No. Unfortunately it was a tragedy that was felt equally by all of us. It wasn't Matt's fault, my fault, or the boy's fault. Well, maybe Keisha's?

Children can grow up in an environment where they raise themselves, drugs and crime are everywhere, and these kids don't die tragically. Why? Well because it is not about us and what we do. Anyone that has had a two-year-old knows that moment where they say, where is _____? Just to find relief when they are digging in your purse, coloring on the wall, or pooping in the corner. Why some people get to find their children coloring on the wall and others like mine end tragically, I'm not sure. What I do know is that there are no accidents to God. He has a hand in all of life and death.

Choose to take your thoughts captive. God does not want for any of us to be defeated by our circumstances. Guilt, blame and regret will stop you from moving forward and will ultimately bring you down. Choose to live and have faith that God is in control.

I have healed, but it is not over

Although I can say that I have been restored, my grief is not over and probably never will be.

There are longer stretches of time that are good. The moments of peace and laughter are many. Because of that it feels like an even bigger blow when grief creeps back into the forefront of our daily lives.

Unexpected triggers can cause the feelings of sadness to resurface. My grief class referred to these triggers as the feeling of being ambushed. One can be fine in a moment and then all of a sudden the situation can completely consume you with emotions. You cannot plan for this grief. It sometimes happens in places where you would rather it not. It is just part of the unpredictable road of grief.

Thoughts of Emma surge at different times with many who were close to her. I was driving Jayden to baseball practice one day and something triggered his thoughts of Emma. He said, "You know, I would do anything if I could bring Emma back. I would even climb on the highest building there is and I'm even afraid of heights! But I would do it for her." It is a reminder to me that although the boys continue to thrive in school and with sports, their grief for Emma is not gone and probably will never be.

Tyler was angry at home and at school for a period. I later learned that he was reading "Bridge to Terabithia" in school. The book triggered his grief for Emma as a character in the book, a ten-year-old girl in the story drowns. He felt as if he were carrying the weight of the world. Once we talked it out and he had a good cry, he was back to himself. He had been ambushed; completely unable to escape the grief of the situation. His grief had been suppressed and that translated into anger. Once he was able to cry and release his grief, he became more pleasant at home and at school; the Tyler we knew.

Spring and baseball season bring out the feelings of grief in our family. We enjoy baseball, Matt enjoys coaching, but there is an obvious void on the bench next to me. He had looked forward to coaching her as well. Emma's friends are still there, but she is not. The season for us will never be what it was; only what it is now. Some days we are fine, and others we are taken over with emotions.

Recently we went through some of my dad's things and pictures from my childhood. As I looked at pictures of myself at three and four years old, I could see a resemblance to Emma. I could see what she might look like, be like. I want to know why I don't get to see that. I had a surge of emotions. My dad used to sing to me and one song in particular, called "Hold on to the Years". I found the lyrics when we were cleaning. Here is the chorus:

And it seems like yesterday when you first came our way
The answer to an honest, fervent prayer,
I hope someday you'll see that I was all I knew to be
Since the time the Father placed you in our care
When my prayers you cannot hear,
When I'm not there to dry your tears
I trust that you will hold on to the years.

The feelings of grief from my dad and grief from Emma surged. The loss of my past and loss of my future have collided and I am stuck in the present. A very complicated state of grief has found me aside from all of the progress I have made.

I suppose the reason that I am sharing this is that I think it is important to know that although we persevere, although we succeed, although we look better, we are still broken. If you are still broken, it is not failure. It is part of the journey and it takes time, perhaps a lifetime.

Yes, I have healed but it is not over.

Part 5
Restoration and Hope

Be of good courage, and He shall strengthen
your heart, all you who hope in the Lord.
Psalm 31:24

I do not have to be defined by my pain

At one time or another, we will all experience pain. Whether your pain includes loss, abuse, disappointment, abandonment, or something else, we all have a choice. Do we want the pain to be the story of our lives? Essentially do we want to be defined by it?

As for me, I do not want to be defined by the loss of Emma. I am more than the woman who lost her two- year-old. I am multi-dimensional and so are you. Not everything I do in my life, good or bad, is a reflection of my loss.

I am proud to be known as Emma's mom. I am happy to be referenced in that way. But the loss of Emma does not reflect her life and I will work hard to not allow it to reflect mine.

I think when someone allows their pain to take over their life, the pain overshadows everything. God did not intend for us to be defeated by our pain. He desires for us to be conquerors of our difficulties to reflect His love and power for us.

I am still a wife to my husband, a mother to the boys, a teacher in my classroom, a friend, a daughter, a sister, an auntie. I am not *just* the woman who lost her two-year-old.

Hopefully I made an impact in the 35 years here on earth before I had Emma, and hopefully I will make an impact on my life here after losing Emma. Would it be fair then, to conclude that my loss is the whole story? I hope not.

I am still writing my story and so are you. What do want it to say about you?

I recall one evening when my mom and I and the boys were playing a board game. It was a game with questions and answers. My mom's question was, "If there was a song about your life, what would it be?" My heart sank. My mind went to "Memories." Without hesitation, she said, "On the

Road Again". I thought, "Wow, now there is someone who is looking at her whole life, not just the past five years." She had traveled the world and the country with her family, my dad, and countless friends. That is perspective.

What song would represent your life? With God's help, your song, your story, doesn't have to be defined by your pain.

Finding My Place

After our loss, my life was turned upside down and the pieces no longer fit together. Our family ran like a well-oiled machine before with Matt taking the boys to their practices and such, while Emma and I would do our thing.

I found myself alone. Matt would continue to coach and hang with the boys and I had a hard time joining them. Before we had Emma, the four of us did everything together, and after we had her, we would divide and conquer. Now this left me without my part.

I didn't want to sit at baseball practice with empty arms. I didn't want to play football. I would stay home. Matt didn't like me home alone. He would try to encourage me to go with them and be present. He said that it was good for me and for the boys. He reminded me that they still needed me to be active with them. I knew he was right and I took baby steps.

But the boys had become so independent, that it felt like suddenly no one needed me for anything. They shower alone, get dressed alone, they get their own cereal, a little too old and cool to cuddle. What is my role? Where do I fit in?

I would try to go with the boys and one day I walked to the park with them and our dog Keisha. I found myself sobbing and on the way back home. Am I so desperate to have full arms that I will seriously show up with the dog? I hate this new life.

I was trying to recreate the life before we had Emma. The problem is that we did have Emma and we cannot go back to that place. So I had to create a new place, a new fit.

Just as I was feeling like I didn't "fit" anymore, Miss Ronda, our friend and Emma's childcare provider gave our family a trip to a cabin in Pine Crest for a week. I knew this trip meant something. I knew that this was an opportunity to "rejoin" and accept my new role. That is exactly what it was. It snowed heavily. It was beautiful! We played in the snow, built snowmen, sipped hot chocolate day and night, and so much more. We played board games, twister, and air hockey. There were no distractions. It was our family, our new family of four. We still talk of that trip, and the boys refer to it as the best vacation ever! I know that it was more than vacation. It was life-changing. Thank you Nana.

There is something to be said for putting yourself out there and just doing it. I didn't feel like it for a long time, but eventually it did become my fit again. These days showing up alone with empty arms is not as painful as it was before. It is my new reality. It is actually becoming more familiar each day.

The boys do need me. Perhaps they don't want to sit on my lap anymore, and they die of embarrassment when I try to kiss them in public, but they are still little boys who need their mama.

I didn't sign up for adolescence. I'd prefer toddler issues to hormones. The bottom line is this is where I am at so I might as well give adolescence my best. As I've begun to embrace these ages and stages, I have to say that I am beginning to really enjoy where they are now.

My old life is not a choice for me, but finding my place in my new life is. I will continue to search for doing what is the best I can do with the situation I have been dealt. I am proud of my boys and I love supporting their endeavors. I have to be present in these new moments with them because they too are fleeting. I don't want to look back one day and think, "Wow I was in a fog all those years."

I believe that I have found my place in my home once again. Saying "family of four" when putting our name in at a restaurant isn't as painful as it was before. I am thankful for this family of four that I have. It is my place.

Special days and keeping their memory alive

Although holidays and special days can bring about emotions related to missing our loved ones, it also gives us a time to think of them more deeply and reflect on what they meant in our lives.

When thinking of my dad or Emma during the holidays, I think of what I loved and shared about having them during those times. I choose not to stay in the place of "My life is ruined and this holiday will never be good again." It really is a choice on perspective.

I think of my dad singing Blue Christmas and watching football. I think of Emma rocking and hushing her new baby dolls and getting on her new rocking horse. I think of Emma anticipating Santa and saying "ho ho ho" at age one. It makes me smile. It might bring a tear to my eye, but that just demonstrates my love for her. It really does not have to be a negative time.

To honor Emma's birthday each year, my mom and I will host a "Bead for Life" party. All of the proceeds go to benefit women and children in Uganda who are poverty stricken. I can honor Emma's life by helping someone else in her name. I cannot buy Emma a gift anymore. I can take my efforts and place them elsewhere.

My friend Daphne gave me some little "Random act of kindness cards". This has been a fun way to honor her life. On the card it says, "This random act of kindness was done in memory of _____." I can write her name and make someone else's day in her memory.

There is the place in our house where some of her pictures and things are displayed. She did live in our house and she will always be a part of us and our house. I think it honors her by looking at her cute face every day. Some days

148

that is painful, but for me it is more comforting than hiding her things and acting like she never existed.

Soon after Emma died, Jayden wrote a song about her titled, "Emma Grace". He gave his little song a tune. (He must take after his dad) One night when Katie was babysitting she recorded him singing it. I took the recording to "Build- a- Bear" and placed the recording of his song into a stuffed doggie that we named "Big Brother Dawg". That moment was captured and we gave him the dog for his birthday.

After the first year when I had to go through her things and decide what to keep and what not to keep, I decided to make two photo books; one of her first year and one of her second year. When my dad died, I made a little scrapbook as well. It helps to finalize memories when they are organized. It also ensures that all the priceless memories are together in one place so there is no fear in losing something.

I have some special jewelry that I wear on some days to keep her close to me. There are many different ways to honor your loved ones. I heal best when I am active in my healing. Once I have gone through her things, once everything is as it should be, once she has a tree at Christmas for example, and I have special things that make me feel close to her…at that time, I need to accept it and know in my heart that I have done everything I can do for her. It makes the special days and holidays to come more bearable because there is no unfinished business. At that time, I can focus on what this year's holidays bring and not dwell on all of the past holidays that I wish were still here.

Facing the Future

*Jeremiah 29:11 "For I know the plans I have for you,"
declares the Lord, Plans to prosper you and not to harm you,
plans to give you hope and a future."*

Soon after losing Emma, I thought I would never be
happy again. I remember sitting in a grief support group and
stating, "People who go on to have more kids can find hope,
but not me." This is it for me. I have nothing to look forward
to. I completely doubted that I would ever be happy again. I
knew I would be ok. I knew I would continue to raise my
boys and work, but that felt like settling to me. Those
feelings were very real and were in the depths of my grief.

After the first year I began to see some glimpses of joy
once again, but still not restoration. I pondered my future. I
couldn't see how my future would ever be fulfilling again. I
was able to recognize that I would have happy moments with
the boys, that I would celebrate in their milestones. It didn't
feel the same though as being satisfied.

During the summer after the first year, when I had
expected restoration, I couldn't fathom a happy future. I
thought, "Nope, I just get to watch everyone else enjoy their
lives. Yeah for me! The happiest moments of my life are
over."

As we progressed through the second year, Matt and I
tried to "move on" by buying happiness. We bought new
couches. I bought new clothes. I started to take better care of
myself. We started going out. We began to drink wine
regularly. We tried to make the best of our lives by having
fun. Sad times were behind us and we were just going to live
richly! Well, you can only have so many scarves and then
what? You can only go out to dinner so many times and then

what? The night scene is fun at first, but then what? Hmmm, so we can't buy our happiness? Darn it!

Back to the drawing board to plot out our futures! Well, Tyler wants to go to the University of Oregon (Go Ducks!) when he turns 18, so at least one of us has a plan. As I write this book, I feel like it is therapy but not future sustaining happiness. I ponder continuing my education. The problem is that no professional success will fulfill me. I am not the type of person who needs accolades or feels important with rankings. I suppose I can travel or take up a new hobby but most of those things bring temporary satisfaction. So what is the thing that will fulfill me once again?

Today I cannot think of anything that will be as fulfilling as being a mom. No success, no worldly gains will do it for me. Our quest to adopt is getting further away as the bureaucracy and financial stress sadly turns us off. We have considered the vasectomy reversal more than ever before. Honestly, we wanted a miracle. We even expected one. Faith of a mustard seed, huh? This is where faith meets science, and miracles meet medicine. I suppose sometimes the work and the pain involved to achieve your dreams is part of the journey.

As we face our futures without our loved ones, it is easy to feel hopeless. I have peace. I can live a status quo life, but I want more! I am a dreamer. You and I need to search our hearts and pray for restoration. God will restore us each differently. My future has purpose and meaning and I need to seek what that is for me, and perhaps so do you.

I will raise a toast (and a prayer) to my future and yours. To a future with hope and possibility!

Acceptance and Hope- Your loved one's legacy

Proverbs 23:18 "There is surely a future hope for you, and your hope will not be cut off."

1 Corinthians 13:13 "And now these three remain: faith, hope, and love"

"All is well with your little child because she is in the presence of God the Father in absolute perfection"
Luis Palau

As time passes and we have done all that we can do, we must accept our new lives. I would've written my life differently. Whether or not I like the portion that has been dealt to me doesn't change what is. We must learn to accept it. Once we accept it, we can hope for a new future. We hope that we will be restored. We hope that we will see our loved ones again. We hope that good will come out of tragedy.

When we fully accept the magnitude of our loss and once we not only hope for a day to be reunited with them, but count on it, we can begin to develop a legacy in their memory.

Emma shined her light in her little life. Although her light was bright, my actions after her loss could affect her legacy. I want her legacy to be "shine even in darkness" so I choose to live that in her honor. If I allowed her loss to destroy me, then that would overshadow the light she was. We are a huge part in carrying out our loved ones legacies.

What is your loved ones legacy? How do you want people to remember them? I don't want my behavior to fog the views of my daughter's life. She was beautiful. She was simple. She was funny. She was a peace-maker. And she had a light that would draw others to her.

What will your legacy be? What will people say about you? What do want them to say? Each day we have choices; big choices and little choices. All of our choices will become part of our stories, our legacies.

Emma's legacy reminds me of the song, "This little light of mine". So child-like, so Emma, just simple and profound. If you would like to honor her and yourselves, shine your lights! Shine your lights in the good days and in the bad days, in the darkness and the light.

Living Large

Throughout this season in our lives, we have had the desire to continue to live, and in fact, to not just live, but to live large! As a family, we have experienced life in a very large way despite our grief. We have been surprised at some of the events and accomplishments that have transpired during the lowest point in our lives. The events below all occurred during 2011-2012; the first year after losing Emma.

Tyler All Star

The Price is Right!

Matt receives Employee of the Year

Tyler wins 4th place in a state
Basketball competition

154

My Teacher of the Year honor

Jayden is named MVP

Tyler becomes a trumpet player

Jayden receives a county Art Award

Because He Lives

Hymn Written by Bill and Gloria Gaither

God sent His son, they called Him **Jesus.**
He came to **love, heal** and **forgive.**
He lived and died to **buy my pardon**.
An empty grave is there to prove my Savior **lives!**

Because He lives **I can face tomorrow.**
Because He lives **all fear is gone.**
Because I know **he holds the future.**
And that makes **life worth the living** because He lives.

How sweet to **hold a newborn baby,**
And feel the pride and **joy he gives.**
But greater still the **calm assurance**
This child **can face uncertain days** because **He lives.**

And then one day **I'll cross the river,**
I'll fight **life's final war** with **pain.**
And then as **death** gives way to **victory,**
I'll see the lights of glory and I'll know He lives!

So for all of you that wonder and ask me how I do it each
day? Here is the answer.

Because He Lives

*This is an old hymn that I remember my dad singing. It offers
full hope!*
*The woman who wrote this was pregnant with her third child
as her husband struggled with a chronic illness. The words
of surrender landed on the pages. I'm glad they did.*

In Full Bloom

I hesitate to write that I have arrived. I know that my love and my grief for Emma will always be with me. I have grown a lot though, in my grief, in my faith, and with my purpose.

God has restored me. I can even say that I truly am a happy person again. That is not ordinary for someone in my situation. God has taken the ordinary and turned it into extraordinary. I know that the peace in my soul is because of God. I know that the perspective I carry about life and death is because of God's promises.

There have been several indicators of blooming in our lives. The boys continue to thrive in school, with sports, and with everything they do. Is that normal for grief-stricken children? No. I have prayed and God has made provisions for their restoration. Amazing! My perky self has shown herself more these days too. I remember one incident where I got into an argument with someone over something silly. I walked away saying, "YES! My spunk is back!" Not to say that that is a good trait, but I felt the old Heather again. When in the depths of grief, I never had the emotional strength to debate, argue, or even care for that matter. And now I am stronger.

Today I was looking through some of Emma's things and I was crying. Jayden was looking for me and he found me. He looked into my eyes. He hugged me. He looked down and smiled and said, "Remember that time-out chair? Good times, good times!" We both laughed and continued with our morning. Memories, sadness, progress and laughter can co-exist. They probably always will.

Tyler is becoming a young man with incredible strength. He has been able to hold his head high recently with confidence. He displays honesty with his grief and a perseverance that makes me proud. His character has been tested and God is chiseling him for His purpose. Could a mom hope for anything more?

Evidence of blooming was around during football season this year as well. I am a Saints fan. I watched, clapped, and yelled at every game on TV. I wore my Saints shirt and donned a license plate cover on my car. I know this represents progress, because the year after Emma's death, I took my license plate cover off of my car. I remember thinking, "I can't display something that 'unimportant' on my vehicle. Nope. A football fan is shallow." Well shallow or not, I'm back! And it feels good! Who Dat???

The peace Matt and I share with one another and our families has bloomed. We believe that there is absolutely purpose to tragedy. We will continue to look for the good. We will continue to be thankful for what we have and not focus on what we don't.

Blooming… I am blooming! My petals are back! Thank you God for helping me to Bloom!

Closing and Reflection

I did not sign up for this journey, however, I'm not sure that I could have demonstrated God's love, faithfulness, and the strength He gives us had I not been on this journey. It is difficult for me to end this story because I continue to change and grow. This story represents a time.

Ecclesiastes 3 says, "There is a time for everything, and a season for every activity under heaven."

Am I thankful for this time? Not really. But some days I feel honored that God has trusted me with this story. Some days I am grateful to be the one who gets to choose to not be defeated. On other days, I will still whine, "Why me?" On days when I'm missing Emma more than normal, I still wish this wasn't my portion.

I can't say that prior to losing Emma, I'd ever felt like I "needed God", desperately needed God. I chose God. I chose to be faithful, but that is different than needing Him. Having experienced this has given me a deeper dependency on Him.

Our choices really do change our outcomes. In the end it comes down to grace. I can choose to live out the rest of my life with dignity and grace. I can pray to be clothed in peace. I can pray for wisdom to continue to parent the boys. I can count on the strength that God promises us.

Hopefully something in this book has touched your heart. By sharing Emma's life and death with you, my prayer is that each of you recognizes your life as a gift each day. I also pray that each of you draws to a deeper dependency on God. I'm not talking about religion. I'm not talking about church. I'm talking about your heart.

In John 14 verses 5 and 6, Thomas was asking Jesus about heaven. He said, "Lord we do not know where you are going, how will we know the way?" Jesus answered, "I am the way and the truth and the life. No one comes to Father except through me."

Thank you for taking this journey with me; A new day is coming, and I will continue to pray for all of the broken hearts out there that need mending. Life is hard sometimes. In our hard moments we have the ability to shine more than ever if we choose to!

Family days one week before

The Fourth of July- a family tradition

July 6, 2010

Pictures taken less than an hour before our lives changed forever…

Emma's grave marker

The place we must visit her now.

"He will wipe every tear from their eyes. There will be no more death or mourning or crying or pain, for the old order of things has passed away." Revelation 21:4

Suggested Resources

Books

David W. Wiersbe, *Gone, But not Lost, Grieving the Death of a Child*, 1992
Jerry Bridges, *Trusting God Even when Life Hurts, 1988*
Dr. James Dobson, *When God Doesn't Make Sense*, 1993
Erwin Lutzer, *One Minute After You Die*, 1997
Erwin Lutzer, *The Vanishing Power of Death*, 2004
Jeremy Camp, I Still Believe, 2011
Joey O' Connor, Children and Grief- Helping Your Child Understand Death, 2004
H. Norman Wright, It's Okay to Cry- A Parent's Guide to helping children through the losses of life, 2004

CD's

Mercy Me- Undone
Jeremy Camp- I Still Believe
Matthew West- The Story of your Life
Chris Tomlin- And if our God is For Us; Arriving
Sidewalk Prohets- These Simple Truths
Sanctus Real- Pieces of a Real Heart
Steven Curtis Chapman- Beauty Will Rise
Casting Crowns-Until the Whole World Hears

Grief Support Groups

Grief Share www.griefshare.org or call 800-395-5755 for a group in your area
Compassionate Friends www.compassionatefriends.org/

I would like to extend some special thanks. One to my family, my mom and my sisters whose continual love and support means the world to me! And to my friend Anna Mayer, who captured our little girl through photographs without us even knowing! (The cover photo and several in this book) Thanks Anna! I'd like to thank Major Mitchell, the publisher, whose faith in this project from the beginning I am grateful for. Also, to Karen Borrelli, for her patience with me in the design and formatting of this book. Thank-you!

Finally to my friend Lisa Travis (Colie's mom) whose constant feedback, push and encouragement motivated me to finish this in Emma's honor. Thanks Lisa! And to my dad, who has now met Emma, who taught me to put Christ first in all things…even bad, yucky things. Thanks dad. Love you!

Just Bloom...... Emma

About The Author

Heather Vargas has been an elementary school teacher for 16 years. She was 2011's Gustine Unified School District Teacher of the Year. Heather loves advocating for students who have not yet found their voice. She currently works at Gustine Intermediate School as an Academic Coach. She resides in Newman, California with her husband Matt and her two boys, Tyler and Jayden who in her eyes are the best part of life.

Contact Information

For the journey continued, please follow my blog at
http://bloomvargas.wordpress.com

You may also e-mail me at bloomvargas@gmail.com

For your reading pleasure, we invite you to visit our Trading Post bookstore.

Children's Books

Beam
Charlie Shepherd
The Witch On Oak Street
Were You Born In That Chair?

Novels

The Doña
Mokelumne Gold
Poverty Flat
Dusty Boots
A Reason To Believe
Desperado Moon
Time Will Tell
Never Give Up

Shalako Press

http://www.shalakopress.com

CPSIA information can be obtained at www.ICGtesting.com
Printed in the USA
LVOW010819051112

305847LV00001B/1/P